NEWMAN'S *Apologia*: A CLASSIC RECONSIDERED

NEWMAN'S *Apologia:* A CLASSIC RECON-SIDERED -- *edited by Vincent Ferrer Blehl, S.J., and Francis X. Connolly* --- HARCOURT, BRACE & WORLD, INC., NEW YORK ~

NIHIL OBSTAT: *Edward J. Montano, S.T.D., Censor Librorum*
IMPRIMATUR: ✠ *Francis Cardinal Spellman, Archibishop of New York*

The nihil obstat and imprimatur are official declarations that a book or pamphlet is free of doctrinal or moral error. No implication is contained therein that those who have granted the nihil obstat and imprimatur agree with the contents, opinions or statements expressed.

FIRST EDITION

Library of Congress Catalog Card Number: 64-18283

PRINTED IN THE UNITED STATES OF AMERICA

PREFACE

To commemorate the centenary of the publication of John Henry Newman's classic *The Apologia Pro Vita Sua,* the Fordham University Center of Newman Studies sponsored a symposium on October 12, 1963. The eight papers are presented here, together with a bibliography, in the hope that they will make the *Apologia* better known not only to the student but also to the general reader.

In a sense the *Apologia* is one of the most difficult of the acknowledged English classics. It grew out of a complicated history involving the Oxford Movement, the rise of liberalism, the deterioration of Church-State relations in Great Britain, the restoration of the Catholic hierarchy, the rise and fall of ecclesiastical factions and personalities. Its argument presupposes some knowledge of theology and philosophy, both in themselves and in their relation to ancient councils, debates and historical upheavals. Its language is that of the classic philosophers and poets, of the Fathers of the Church, medieval doctors, seventeenth-century English divines, and of nineteenth-century Oxford common rooms. Its immediate occasion, Charles Kingsley's charge that Newman had no respect for truth, leads to a labyrinth of assertions and counter-assertions based on the interpretation of writings whose contexts must be carefully explored. Small wonder, then, that the modern reader approaches the *Apologia* with a degree of timidity that often deprives him of that uninhibited experience which is the proper reward of his reading.

Within the limitations imposed by the occasion, this volume attempts to lessen this timidity by considering the *Apologia* freshly in terms of its history, its literary characteristics, and its theological and philosophical implications.

Historical perspective is the principal concern of the first three essays. Martin Svaglic's review of the critical controversy with Charles Kingsley leads up to an analysis of the issues of that dispute and a re-examination of the reasons why Newman wrote the *Apologia*. Professor Svaglic is chiefly concerned with Newman's defense of himself and the Catholic position in general against Anglican and Protestant charges of insincerity. Dr. Edward Kelly on the other hand shows how Newman also wrote with an eye on the special objections of conservative, ultramontane Catholics to his view of the Catholic Church. Professor Blehl's analysis of the early critics of the *Apologia* uncovers a wide spectrum of criticism, none of it comprehensive, some of it ambivalent, much of it contingent upon the religious bias of the reviewer. As a result of his survey Father Blehl raises an interesting critical question: How can those critics who affirm that

Newman's self-analysis was misguided also maintain that the *Apologia* is a psychological masterpiece?

The essays in the next group deal chiefly with literary aspects of the *Apologia*. Dean Buckler addresses himself to the problem of the present-day reader of the *Apologia* who is unacquainted with the history and theology of the *Apologia*. His main point is that within the historical and theological framework Newman has provided a rich human experience mediated through a style of extraordinary artistry. Sister Mary Baylon Lenz explores Newman's literary art with particular attention to its ethical appeal. Newman's ethical argument (in Aristotle's words, the speech spoken so as "to make us think the speaker credible") is revealed in the basic structure of the *Apologia*. Sister Mary Baylon shows how Newman strove to establish the image of his loyalty to Anglicanism at every point in his career. Professor Connolly's essay shows that the *Apologia* is a work of history and of rhetoric but also, and more importantly, a spiritual autobiography marked by unity of theme, a self-revealing style, and an unusual mastery of perspective and tone.

Since Newman merely narrated his intellectual history and described, rather than justified, his theological and philosophical views, the *Apologia* cannot be considered a tract. Yet it does contain important theological and philosophical implications. As Father Hugo de Achaval points out, Newman's emphasis on the "real" knowledge of God, in conscience and in the doctrine of the Incarnation—views that he subsequently explained in detail in *The Grammar of Assent* and in the 1878 edition of the *Essay on the Development of Christian Doctrine*—also permeate the theology of the *Apologia*. In the *Apologia* these ideas are seen as an inner dynamism, reflecting the genesis and development of Newman's thought. Similarly, Father Jonathan Robinson shows how Newman's process of reasoning, explained with more detail and precision in *The Grammar of Assent*, is manifested informally in the *Apologia*.

A symposium, however successful, can only open doors to the many meanings and mysteries contained in a book as rich as the *Apologia*. If this small tribute to a great classic does just that its sponsors will be grateful. For those who wish to explore further, Sister Mary James, O.P., has supplied a bibliography.

The editors wish to thank their collaborators, all of whom interrupted important work to contribute to this symposium. They are also most grateful to the librarians of Fordham University, Dr. Joseph Hart and Miss Ann Murphy, who greatly aided their work by providing microfilm copies of original Newman materials and to the Fathers of the Oratory in Birmingham, England.

Vincent Ferrer Blehl, S.J.
Francis X. Connolly
FORDHAM UNIVERSITY
January 1964

CONTENTS

Martin J. Svaglic: WHY NEWMAN WROTE THE *Apologia*

On December 30, 1863, Newman received in the mail a copy of *Macmillan's Magazine* for January, 1864, containing an enthusiastic review, signed "C.K.," of volumes seven and eight of James Anthony Froude's ultra-Protestant *History of England*. Certain passages had been marked by the sender, who later identified himself as William Pope, a former Anglican clergyman.[1] In the course of a sharp attack by the reviewer on the injury done to Catholic moral standards by the growth of papal authority, Newman read:

It was not till more than one generation had grown up and died with the Bible in their hands, that Englishmen and Germans began to understand (what Frenchmen and Italians did not understand) that they were to be judged by the everlasting laws of a God who was no respecter of persons.

And then came the words soon to become familiar throughout England:

> So, again, of the virtue of truth. Truth, for its own sake,
> had never been a virtue with the Roman clergy. Father Newman
> informs us that it need not, and on the whole ought not to be;
> that cunning is the weapon which Heaven has given to the
> Saints wherewith to withstand the brute male force of the
> wicked world which marries and is given in marriage. Whether
> his notion be doctrinally correct or not, it is at least historically
> so.[2]

What followed is so well known as to require only a
brief summary here. All the relevant documents may be
found in several editions of the *Apologia*.[3] Without asking
any redress, Newman at once called the attention of Messrs.
Macmillan to "a grave and gratuitous slander" for which no
justification from any words of his had been offered. This
was the heart of Newman's objection. From first to last, in
all the correspondence that followed after Charles Kingsley
identified himself as the writer (to Newman's professed
amazement [4]), Kingsley could not be brought to cite any
specific words of Newman in support of his categorical accusation. He first proposed an insinuating apology which
only aggravated the original injury by such remarks as "No
man knows the use of words better than Dr. Newman; no
man, therefore, has a better right to define what he does,
or does not, mean by them." But neither then nor in the
brief apology he published in the February number of *Macmillan's* (modified after Newman objected to the passage
quoted and one other) did he offer any evidence for his
charge beyond a general reference to Newman's Anglican
sermon "Wisdom and Innocence." Yet he persisted in referring to Newman's "words."

The fact is that Kingsley could find no specific words

to prove his charge, for, as his latest biographer says, "what Newman had preached was quite the reverse" of Kingsley's report:

In describing the weapons with which the Christian Church defends itself, prayer, holiness, and innocence, he had said that to the world of physical strength these weapons were so incomprehensible that it must believe that the Church conquered by craft and hypocrisy. "The words 'craft' and 'hypocrisy,' are but the version of 'wisdom' and 'harmlessness,' in the language of the world." [5]

Yet, as events were to prove, Kingsley had no intention of giving up his charge, as against Newman or the Catholic priesthood. He was either too proud to confess on the one hand that he could not find a definite passage in the sermon to justify his accusation, or reluctant to admit on the other that he had not fundamentally changed his mind about the justice of it. In his pamphlet answering Newman's, he was to explain his failure to back up his charge in detail by saying that he "had been informed (by a Protestant) that Newman was in weak health, that he wished for peace and quiet, and was averse to controversy." [6]

Newman had warned Kingsley from the start of their correspondence that he would consider his letters public property, and Kingsley admitted that he had "every right to do so." Having failed to get any real satisfaction for the gratuitous and wholesale slander, Newman at first thought of putting his correspondence with Kingsley in an appendix to the next edition of *The Present Position of Catholics in England*, as he had earlier done with his correspondence on miracles with the Bishop of Norwich, who had attacked Newman's view.[7]

However, the reply of his friend Edward Badeley, a

distinguished lawyer, to Newman's question as to whether Badeley considered Kingsley's original apology sufficient, apparently led him to change his mind. "Such an apology, I think," wrote Badeley, "would not be deemed sufficient in any Court of justice, or in any society of gentlemen; I have no hesitation in declaring, that I consider it a disgrace to the writer. . . ." And he presently added: "I think that he deserves a most severe castigation." [8]

By late January, Newman had decided to publish the correspondence at once. It appeared on February 12 as a pamphlet called *Mr. Kingsley and Dr. Newman: A Correspondence on the Question whether Dr. Newman Teaches That Truth Is No Virtue?* Appended were Newman's ironical "Reflections" in the form of a dialogue turning Kingsley's charge back upon himself:

Mr. Kingsley relaxes: "Do you know, I like your *tone*. From your tone I rejoice, greatly rejoice, to be able to believe that you did not mean what you said."

I rejoin: "*Mean* it! I maintain I never *said* it, whether as a Protestant or as a Catholic."

Mr. Kingsley replies: "I waive that point."

I object: "Is it possible? What? Waive the main question! I either said it or I didn't. You have made a monstrous charge against me; direct, distinct, public. You are bound to prove it as directly, as distinctly, as publicly;—or to own you can't."

"Well," says Mr. Kingsley, "if you are quite sure you did not say it, I'll take your word for it; I really will."

My *word!* I am dumb. Somehow I thought that it was my *word* that happened to be on trial. The *word* of a Professor of lying, that he does not lie!

But Mr. Kingsley re-assures me. "We are both gentlemen," he says: "I have done as much as one English gentleman can expect from another."

I begin to see: he thought me a gentleman at the very

time that he said I taught lying on system. After all, it is not I, but it is Mr. Kingsley who did not mean what he said.

Newman concluded his pamphlet by expressing the feeling that the correspondence lying between Mr. Kingsley's "January enormity" and his "miserably insufficient" February explanation constituted "a real satisfaction to those principles of historical and literary justice to which he has given so rude a shock. Accordingly I have put it into print, and make no further criticism on Mr. Kingsley." [9]

If Kingsley had had the wisdom to accept this stinging but merited rebuke, he might well have come off with a large measure of public sympathy as the almost helpless victim of a hypersensitive and certainly none too popular man variously likened during the progress of the controversy to a lion, an ape, a bear, and a serpent. The *Saturday Review* of February 27, 1864, which heralded the controversy as the liveliest since the days of Bentley and Boyle, described Newman as "the old lion" rousing himself in his den, and concluded with a picture of one remaining for the most part in serene solitude and peaceful rest, "but springing out now and then with the lithe and supple crash of the serpent, erect, defiant, and pitiless, and hissing with scorn, when the hour of vengeance arrived and a helpless victim were within reach of his cruel fangs." [10] And the week before, the literary editor of the *Spectator*, R. H. Hutton, had spoken of Kingsley as a perhaps "too helpless victim" of Newman's "undue scorn" and of a "more than adequate literary retribution." [11]

But the reviewers said other things as well. They said that Newman was fundamentally in the right, and they said things more unflattering to Kingsley than anything in Newman's pamphlet. Hutton, whose opinion carried all the more weight as coming from a known admirer of Kingsley, more than anyone else prepared the way for Newman's

critical and popular rehabilitation by the extensive publicity
he gave to every stage of the controversy and by the pro-
gressively warmer admiration for Newman which he dis-
played. The other major reviewers appear to have followed
his lead.[12]

Loose Thoughts for Loose Thinkers was the unfortunate
subtitle of one of Kingsley's works. According to Hutton,
it represented only

too closely the character of his rough but manly intellect, so
that a more opportune Protestant ram for Father Newman's
sacrificial knife could scarcely have been found . . . the thicket
in which he caught himself was, as it were, of his own choosing,
he having rushed into it, quite without malice, but also quite
without proper consideration of the force and significance of his
own words. Mr. Kingsley is really without any case at all . . .
and we think that he drew down upon himself fairly the last
keen blow of the sacrificial knife by what we must consider a
very inadequate apology for his rash statement.[13]

The *Saturday Review* was more cutting:

Mr. Kingsley's habit of mind is a very unfortunate one for a
serious investigator of truth. He is only deficient in the accom-
plishments of accuracy and gravity. To weigh his words is not so
important as to calculate their force. Lively, impetuous, vigorous, hasty, too quick in forming judgments and too vehement
in expressing them, he is a brilliant partisan but a very unsafe
teacher . . . he is apt to be careless in investigating the grounds
of what ought to be his judgments, but which are his prejudices.
He is the most sensational writer of history who ever disdained
the labour of reading.[14]

Newman's pamphlet created a small literary sensation. In the
first impression only 500 copies had been run off, but these
were exhausted almost immediately; and in less than two
months 1,737 copies were sold.[15]

Even rasher than before, smarting under such an attack, and badly advised by friends, Kingsley began his extraordinary reply. "I am answering Newman now," he wrote to a correspondent, "and though of course I give up the charge of conscious dishonesty, I trust to make him and his admirers sorry that they did not leave me alone. I have a score of more than twenty years to pay, and this is an installment of it." [16] On March 20 he published his pamphlet *What, Then, Does Dr. Newman Mean?*

Even today, after a hundred years, anyone reading this work for the first time will be startled by the passionate intensity and bitterness of Kingsley's attack on Newman. "I struck as hard as I could," he later admitted.[17] The bluntness of language and confusion of purpose which have given the pamphlet its reputation even among Kingsley's admirers for "bad logic and hot-headed obtuseness" [18] are evident from the start: "I have declared Dr. Newman to have been an honest man up to the 1st of February, 1864. It was, as I shall show, only Dr. Newman's fault that I ever thought him to be anything else. It depends entirely on Dr. Newman whether he shall sustain the reputation which he has so recently acquired." [19] The crude innuendo was proof enough that Newman had rightly judged the sincerity of the apology he had been offered.

For the rest, the pamphlet is from the very title page a farrago of passages torn from the carefully qualified context of Newman's sermons of 1843, "Wisdom and Innocence" and "The Apostolical Christian"; of actual misstatements, as in Kingsley's claim that he was so far just to Newman "that No. 90, which made all the rest of England believe him a dishonest man, had not the same effect on me," a claim flatly contradicted by early letters to his future wife Fanny Grenfell and to his mother; [20] of blatant appeals to prejudice and nationalism ("Englishmen know how to guard the women whom God has committed to their charge"); and in general of the outraged protests of a simple, bluff common sense against the knave or fool who could adapt the system of unnatural asceticism, wild legends, and crafty ethics that Newman had upheld even before joining the church that had spawned it.

Even by those who believed, with Kingsley's friend and brother-in-law J. A. Froude, that in some of Newman's thought there was in fact a sophistical element in need of criticism, there was scarcely an attempt to defend so unfortunate an outburst.[21] As the *London Review* of April 2 observed, describing Kingsley's "furious answer in forty pages to Father Newman's single sheet": ". . . that Mr. Kingsley in his last pamphlet has himself lost his temper, we believe, will be seen by anyone who wades through it, and does not mind being privy to the edifying spectacle of a robust Christian in a rage, exhausting himself in the vain attempt to swear without standing committed to profane language." The reviewer added that Kingsley still had not produced a passage to support his original charge. He "aggravates the original injustice a hundredfold," said R. H. Hutton, and "has done himself pure harm by this rejoinder." [22]

Before the end of March, Newman had begun his reply. He first thought of putting it into lecture form, as Ambrose St. John had strongly urged, but decided that he could not read out a history of his religious opinions.[23] His *Apologia Pro Vita Sua*, a title he probably chose for its patristic echoes, would reveal "that living intelligence by which I write, and argue, and act" [24] as the most effective answer possible to Kingsley's question "What does Dr. Newman mean?" Published by Longmans at Newman's expense, it appeared in seven pamphlets on consecutive Thursdays between April 21 and June 2, 1864, with an eighth (an appendix called *Answer in Detail to Mr. Kingsley's Accusations*) published two weeks later on June 16.[25]

Newman allowed this interval partly because the last section required more time and partly because he wished to have an opportunity to consider any reply made by Kingsley in the meantime. However, Kingsley's high state of tension, aggravated by the controversy, led his wife to keep him from reading the *Apologia* until it was completed. In private, at least, he had earlier hinted at a crushing reply: "such a revanche as will make [Newman] wince, if any English common sense is left in him, which I doubt." [26] But the reply never appeared. Though feeling that he was still essentially in the right, with "nothing to retract, apologize for, explain," Kingsley wrote to Macmillan on June 8 that he would not put himself a second time "into the power of one who, like a treacherous ape, lifts to you meek & suppliant eyes, till he thinks he has you within his reach, & then springs, gibbering & biting, at your face." [27] According to one of his biographers the ground that Kingsley had taken up "was too hopelessly unsound. He retired therefore into silence, with a reputation permanently damaged." [28] Whether or not this is true, there can be no doubt at all that Newman's reputation, so long under a cloud, had begun to shine with a quite new luster.

At a deeper level, the question remains, Why *did* Newman write the *Apologia*? In effect, John Keble himself had asked as much when he wrote to Newman on April 26, 1864, imploring him "not to be seriously worried by such trash as Mr. Kingsley's" and saying of the pain that Newman was giving himself in writing the book, "I should have

thought it might be spared." Newman should guard his
health, Keble said. "*We* (if I may say) want you, dear
J.H.N.—all Christendom wants you—to take your stand
against the infidelity wch seems to [be] so fast enveloping us
all." [29]

This, of course, was just the kind of work that Newman
longed to do; but by 1864 he knew well that unless he first
vindicated his own name, anything he could do in the future
would have little impact, either among Protestants or Catholics. That is why he could say of the *Apologia* in reply to
Keble, "I have for years wished to write it as a duty." [30]
With his friend R. W. Church he was more explicit:

It has always been on my mind that perhaps some day I should
be called on to defend my honesty while in the Church of England. . . . I have considered that if anyone with his name made
an elaborate charge on me, I was bound to speak.

. . . I know well that Kingsley is a furious foolish fellow,—but
he has a name . . . now he comes out with a pamphlet bring-
ing together a hodge podge of charges against me all about dishonesty. Now friends who know me say: "Let him alone,—no
one credits him," but it is not so. This very town of Birmingham,
of course, knows nothing of me, and his pamphlet on its appearance produced an effect. The evangelical party has always
spoken ill of me, and the pamphlet seems to justify them. The
Roman Catholic party does not know me;—the fathers of our
school boys, the priests, &c., &c., whom I cannot afford to let
think badly of me. Therefore, thus publicly challenged, I must
speak, and, unless I speak strongly, men won't believe me in
earnest.[31]

Did Newman, by publishing the correspondence and
appending his devastating reflections, deliberately goad
Kingsley into spelling out his charges so that Newman could
then seize the opportunity to tell the story he had so long

wanted to tell? The question has been asked before. It is impossible to say for certain, but it would not be surprising if the answer were yes. After all, the *Apologia* does open with the words "I cannot be sorry to have forced Mr. Kingsley to bring out in fulness his charges against me." And though Newman's latest and generally excellent biographer, Miss Meriol Trevor, tells us that at the beginning of the Kingsley episode, "Newman had no autobiographical intentions," [32] this is perhaps not quite the case. He was certainly nursing autobiographical hopes, at any rate, though at first he saw no chance to realize them.

In his early letter to Badeley asking whether he thought Kingsley's proposed reparation sufficient, Newman did not regret Kingsley's charges so much as the fact that such charges did not go far enough: "If they would have gone on, speaking of 'Roman duplicity,' 'St. Alfonso,' or my own delinquence in *act*, such as No. 90, Whately's charge against me of remaining a cypto-papist in the Anglican Church, then I could have written what would have been *worth* writing, both as regards the doctrine of Truth, and my own history. But this apparently is not on the cards." [33] It was to be "on the cards" yet, however, for almost by one of those "special providences" Newman loved to chronicle throughout his life, Kingsley's pamphlet would read as if it had been written according to Newman's own specifications.

When Kingsley's pamphlet, first advertised as *What, Then, Does Dr. Newman Teach?*, was announced, Newman wrote to Badeley that he was looking forward to it as something "for which of course I have prepared myself from the first."

I mean, I never have had an opening to defend myself as to various passages in my life and writings, and I have always looked forward to the possibility of that opening being presented to me.

I have for a long time been attempting to arrange my letters and papers with a view to it. Unluckily I have not yet got further than 1836—and what I shall chiefly want is 1841–1845. However, I must take things as they come.[34]

That Newman could have deliberately forced the impetuous Kingsley's hand is a possibility that puts him for some people in an unattractive, Machiavellian light. But there is no good reason why it should do so. Surely no one who knew the sacrifices Newman had made and the misunderstanding from which he had suffered for over twenty years in the cause of what he believed to be truth, making Kingsley's charge a cruel irony indeed, could begrudge him an opportunity to clear his name, an opportunity which he may well have in some way fashioned as well as found. It was Kingsley, after all, not Newman, who had done the injury. It was Kingsley who had the upper hand in England when he began the attack; and as Miss Trevor points out, it took courage for Newman to deliver before a hostile public the challenge of his own pamphlet.

Newman answered Kingsley because Kingsley had a distinguished name and position in mid-Victorian England, and it is well to remind ourselves of that position. He had lived down the opprobrium attached in some high quarters to his earlier Christian Socialist propaganda; he had become one of the most popular novelists in England with books like *Westward Ho!* and *The Water-Babies*; and his many admirers included Victoria and Albert themselves, who made him chaplain to the Queen, tutor in history to the Prince of Wales, and Professor of Modern History at Cambridge. In many ways he was almost as perfect an embodiment of the Victorian bourgeois ethos as Macaulay had been earlier. In answering him Newman hoped to reach beyond Kingsley to the three groups whose good will he especially wanted to recover.

First, there was that large body of Protestant Englishmen who had begun to distrust Newman as early as 1841. Their distrust had been confirmed not only by Newman's conversion in 1845 to an unpopular, somehow unpatriotic creed, but also by some of his polemical activities for a dozen years before the Kingsley affair. When Kingsley said in his pamphlet that Tract 90 had "made all the rest of England" believe the author "a dishonest man," Newman was well aware of the great measure of truth behind the exaggeration. Tract 90 had been thrown in Newman's face year after year since its appearance, often by well-known figures like the M.P., who once pleaded: "Let us not import the morality of Tract 90 into Parliament." Even as sensitive a man as F. D. Maurice, as late as February 24, 1863, in the course of an attack on Dr. Pusey for his attempt to unseat on the ground of heresy the liberal Professor of Greek, Benjamin Jowett, gravely misrepresented the argument of the Tract by describing Newman in the *Times* as "a man who imputed to the writers of the Articles a slippery and dishonest intention, and said that it could only be defeated by slippery and dishonest practice on the other side."

When Newman remonstrated against such an error of interpretation, Maurice handsomely and publicly apologized,[35] but it was obvious enough that if a sophisticated theologian like Maurice could take such a distorted view of Tract 90, that of the average literate Englishman must have been considerably worse. And Newman could not wholly blame those who misunderstood, for Tract 90 had been written for a very special audience of troubled Anglo-Catholics, and unless its novel and fairly subtle premises were carefully mastered, it would inevitably appear strained at times and craftily sophistical. As Newman himself wrote to Pusey on March 1, 1863, the fact that Tract 90 had been one among other means "of keeping up a high Church party among the English clergy . . . is no reason that you should be dragged through the mud by a composition of mine, which, viewed in the concrete, might have much in it, which had better not have been there." [36]

Newman knew, too, that Kingsley's charge about truth for its own sake being no virtue with the Roman clergy was a commonplace among Protestants of the day. Alexander Macmillan himself, one of the founders of the publishing firm and the X.Y. of Newman's pamphlet, said that he had never imagined that Kingsley's review would give offense, since he thought that everyone would agree that Roman Catholics believed truth to be "a matter of enactment." [37]

And when Kingsley wrote in his pamphlet that there was a strong distrust of priests "who, like Dr. Newman, have turned round upon their mother-Church (I had almost said their mother-country) with contumely and slander," [38] Newman must certainly have recognized the truth in the remark, for he had been told something very similar, both in letters and in print, by Englishmen whom he had unhappily offended only a short time before Kingsley's attack. For years he had been the object of rumors about his impending defection from the Church of Rome. Ordinarily he ignored them. On June 9, 1862, the *Lincolnshire Express* printed a letter reporting that the unhappy Newman "has been lately residing in Paris . . . has become utterly sceptical; and as for believing . . . in the creed of Pope Pius IV . . . he absolutely ridicules it and the Romish persuasion altogether. I fear, Mr. Editor, the present phase of Mr. Newman's mind is as notorious as hopeless. . . ."

The clipping was sent to Newman by a friend and convert, J. Spencer Northcote, who said he knew that Newman ordinarily treated such rumors with "the silent contempt they deserve," but that this one seemed to require some attention since it had been spread by a relative of a nobleman to hinder the conversion of a gentleman whose wife had been received into the Catholic Church only a short time before. On June 17, 1862, Newman sent off to the paper a vigorous denial, only to be answered by the rumor-monger on June 23 with a sneer at Tract 90 and Newman's honesty: ". . . among the writers of the *Tracts for the Times* was one who held they [the 39 Articles] might be subscribed in a non-natural sense. . . . Has Mr. Newman any 'mental reserve' in making his present profession?" [39]

On June 27, 1862, the *Morning Advertiser* printed a story that "Dr. Newman has left or is about to leave the Oratory at Brompton, of which he has been the head for several years . . . this step is the preliminary to his return to the Church of England." Though Newman had never lived at or been head of the Brompton Oratory, the story was quickly taken up by other papers, including the widely read *Globe*, which appears to have printed earlier rumors as well. As Newman's friend William Monsell, who sent him the news, put it: "If you were to write something more eloquent than Demosthenes and more imaginative than Shakespeare ever did, they would not allude to your existence, but such notices of you as this will appear I suppose until the end of the chapter."

Determined to have no more of this, especially at a time when Catholics themselves were already suspicious of his loyalty, Newman fired off a blistering letter to the *Globe* (June 28, 1862) containing a profession of "unclouded faith" in the creed of Rome and adding for those Protestants "always on the lookout for some loophole or evasion in a Catholic's statement of fact":

I do hereby profess *ex animo,* with an absolute internal assent and consent, that Protestantism is the dreariest of possible religions; that the thought of the Anglican service makes me shiver, and the thought of the Thirty-nine Articles makes me shudder. Return to the Church of England! No; 'the net is broken, and we are delivered.' I should be a consummate fool (to use a mild term) if in my old age I left 'the land flowing with milk and honey' for the city of confusion and the house of bondage.

This letter finally stopped the rumors, as Newman intended that it should, but it also backfired on Newman himself. It did indeed seem as if he were turning round on his mother church, as the *Saturday Review* of July 5 pointed out to him: "Whether the dear delight of uttering a corrosive epigram against the religion in which you have spent the best fifty years of life is worth its moral dangers, is another question." Several of the letters that Newman kept protest what one writer called the "great want of charity" in Newman's letter. His friend Charles Crawley of Littlemore implored: "Do my dear friend, do tell me that it is *not* yours. . . ."

On July 3 Newman wrote a letter to the editor of the *Birmingham Daily Post* giving the assurance that he was not "passing any criticism on Protestants generally, or . . . being disrespectful to any persons who were faithful to their religious convictions." The harm had been done, however, not only among foes but even among Anglican friends. It is difficult not to believe that the public and Newman's own reaction to this unfortunate episode, coming so soon before the Kingsley outburst, had something at least to do with the gentle spirit and warmly affectionate tone of the *Apologia* itself.

The second group that Newman almost certainly hoped to reach in the *Apologia* was his former friends and associates at Oxford, the majority of whom he felt (even members of his own family) had made themselves dead to him since his conversion. Newman's move had plunged them into sorrow, and no doubt both their feelings and a sense of duty to their own church made difficult a perpetuation of the old ties. In any event, the poignancy for Newman of the loss of Oxford and the long estrangement from family and friends only became sharper as he began to lose favor with Catholics, too; and only a few months before Kingsley's attack he could write to Keble:

You are always with me a thought of reverence and love, and there is nothing I love better than you, and Isaac, and Copeland, and many others I could name, except Him Whom I ought to love best of all and supremely. May He Himself, Who is the overabundant compensation for all losses, give me His own presence, and then I shall want nothing and desiderate nothing, but none *but* He, *can* make up for the loss of those old familiar faces which haunt me continually.[40]

A chance meeting with his onetime curate Copeland in 1862, which Newman was quick to take advantage of, had begun to thaw the ice even before the *Apologia*, and the irresistible charm of that book did the rest. One of the most satisfying rewards that the *Apologia* brought Newman must have been the many letters of congratulation he received, not only from close friends like Keble, but also from those more alien to his temperament like William Palmer of Worcester and even Provost Hawkins of Oriel, who wrote on June 6, 1864: "Much as I have deplored your separation

from us, my affectionate regard for you has remained un-
diminished." [41] In 1865 there was even at last an invitation
to visit his sister Jemima, though Newman was still too hurt
by the long years of silence to accept it just then.[42]

Finally, Newman wished to reach in the *Apologia* his
fellow Catholics, of whom so many had begun to have
doubts about him that in 1861 the well-known Catholic
publisher Burns could advise that Newman's connection
with any periodical would be dangerous to its success: "The
great objection to Newman . . . is his . . . for one reason
or another, unpopularity." [43] What Newman most wanted
to do he described memorably in 1863:

To aim . . . at improving the condition, the status, of the
Catholic body, by a careful survey of their argumentative basis,
of their position relatively to the philosophy and the character
of the day, by giving them juster views, by enlarging and re-
fining their minds, in one word, by education . . . has been
my line. . . ." [44]

He had tried in high hopes to follow this line with the
Catholic University in Dublin, but Ireland was hardly ready
yet for that ambitious project, the most influential members of the Irish hierarchy gave him little support, and he
returned disillusioned to England in 1858. He began, at
Cardinal Wiseman's request, a translation of the Bible, hop-
ing to consider in a prolegomenon some of the problems
now being raised by the new school of Biblical criticism. But
there was some kind of behind-the-scene trouble, including
pressure on Wiseman by the disaffected London Oratory,
and that project came to a halt for reasons not yet altogether
clear.[45]

In 1859, to save it from condemnation and at the express wish of his bishop, Newman accepted the editorship

of the *Rambler,* a high-level Catholic periodical of liberal tendencies which was already in disfavor with the hierarchy for such remarks as the young Sir John Acton's that although St. Augustine was indeed the greatest Doctor of the West, "he was also the father of Jansenism." [46] In July of that year Newman published an article, "On Consulting the Faithful in Matters of Doctrine," whose underlying purpose was to get across the idea that on such current questions as educational policy laymen should indeed be consulted, and, in short, to initiate the development of what is called today a theology of the laity. Because he spoke of a temporary suspense of the *ecclesia docens* during the Arian controversy, when so many of the bishops wavered or espoused the Arian view, Newman found himself delated to Rome before the year was out. The recent editor of his essay describes its publication as "an act of political suicide from which his career within the Church was never fully to recover; at one stroke he, whose reputation as the one honest broker between the extremes of English Catholic opinion had hitherto stood untarnished, gained the Pope's personal displeasure, the reputation at Rome of being the most dangerous man in England, and a formal accusation of heresy preferred against him by the Bishop of Newport." [47]

Though Newman had by then given up the editorship, the cloud that hung over him darkened still further in 1861 when the *Rambler* took the *other* side on the question of the temporal power of the Pope. This was an act that looked like treason to many Catholics, the majority of whom had rallied to the support of the embattled Pio Nono, fearing with him that religion was in grave danger from the anticlerical Left. The days of strong ultramontanism had arrived, when, as Newman put it, "extreme views alone" were in favor.[48] Newman's reserve on the question of the temporal power—he feared the tendency of Catholics to regard it as a matter of Christian doctrine—was widely regarded as disloyalty. In fact, it was Newman's moderate view which finally prevailed, but meanwhile Newman's reputation suffered from the impetuosity and tactlessness of Acton and Simpson, the *Rambler's* editors.

Newman's ordeal with the ultramontanes is the subject of another essay in the present collection. Suffice it to say here that the *Apologia* was in part, especially in the last chapter, Newman's reply and challenge to them. And that is why the letters of testimonial which he received for the *Apologia* from bodies of Catholic clergy and laity all over the world meant so much to him, as a sign that he spoke the mind of a large and important segment of the Church, that he published them in later editions of the book.

In a journal of these years, Newman poured out his growing sadness. In 1863 he wrote:

I look back on my years at Oxford and Littlemore with tenderness . . . it was the time in which I had a remarkable mission— but how am I changed even in look. . . .

I am noticing all this opposition and distrust, not on their own account, for St. Philip had them abundantly, but because they have (to all appearance) succeeded in destroying my influence and my usefulness. Persons who would naturally look towards me, converts who would naturally consult me, are stopped by some light or unkind word said against me. I am *passé*, in decay, I am untrustworthy. . . .[49]

On the eve of the turning point in his fortunes, he says that "if I could believe it to be God's will, [I] would turn away my thoughts from ever writing anything, and should see, in the superintendence of these boys [at the Oratory school], the nearest return to my Oxford life. . . ."[50] He clearly cannot believe it to be God's will; yet he had always been an occasional writer, and there was no one now to provide him with an occasion. He could never write the story of his life for its own sake. To a friend who asked him for an account, he described it as "a short tale, without adventure, without interest except for myself." [51] He had no intention of simply writing a defense of himself: "theologians and ascetic writers tell us," he once wrote to Acton's assistant Wetherell, "that the perfection of a Christian lies in never pleading his own cause. . . ." But he added: "except when accused of error of faith, for such error is dishonorable to God." His example of such an error was "treachery to the cause of truth." "I think it is the duty of one who has occasion to notice this charge made against him *to be indignant*." [52]

And so when, on December 30, 1863, Newman received in the mail a copy of *Macmillan's Magazine*, accusing him and the Roman clergy in general of making no virtue of truth for its own sake, we can now perhaps more readily imagine how he really felt. There can be no question at all, surely, of the sincerity with which he was to write in 1875, on hearing of Kingsley's death: "As to Mr. Kingsley, much less could I feel any resentment against him, when he was accidentally the instrument in the good Providence of God, by whom I had an opportunity given me, which otherwise I should not have had, of vindicating my character and conduct in my *Apologia*. I have always hoped that by good luck I might meet him, feeling sure there would be no embarrassment on my part, and I said Mass for his soul, as soon as I heard of his death." [53]

To understand fully the genesis of the *Apologia*, one should know, of course, not only why Newman decided to write the book but also why Kingsley attacked him in the first place. The latter is a story of many facets, reflecting both Kingsley's highly individual personality and the outlook of an important group of mid-Victorian writers and thinkers with much in common: the prophet Carlyle, the poet Tennyson, the historian J. A. Froude, the theologian F. D. Maurice, and others. That story, at which I have been able to glance only in passing in the limits of this essay, is, however, better suited to another occasion than the present.

NOTES

1. Under the influence of Newman, he had become a Catholic in 1853, together with his brother and three sisters. See Henry Tristram, "Note au bas d'un grand texte," *La France Franciscaine*, IIIe série, XXII (1939), 38.

2. *Apologia Pro Vita Sua*, ed. Wilfrid Ward (London, 1913), p. 6. All references to the *Apologia* are to this edition.

3. In Ward's; in C. F. Harrold's edition (New York, 1947); in the Modern Library (1950), with an introduction by Anton C. Pegis; and in two paperback editions: Riverside, ed. A. Dwight Culler (1956), and Image Books (1956), with an introduction by Philip Hughes.

4. Kingsley's biographer Robert Bernard Martin considers Newman's protestation of surprise "unflattering either to his candour or to his intelligence" since the review was signed C.K. "and we are told that [Kingsley's] name was listed on the cover of the magazine." (*The Dust of Combat* [London, 1959], pp. 243 and 242.)

5. *Ibid.*, p. 238.

6. *Apologia*, p. 25.

7. Letter to Edward Badeley, Jan. 15, 1864, in MS *Apologia* Letters (3 vols.), I, No. 8, in the Birmingham Oratory.

8. *Ibid.*, I, No. 10.

9. *Apologia*, pp. 20–22.

10. XVII, 255.

11. XXXVII, 206 and 207.

12. This view of Hutton's importance was that of a contemporary critic, G. L. Craik. It has been generally accepted. See Wilfrid Ward, *The Life of John Henry Cardinal Newman* (2 vols., London, 1912), II, 4.

13. The *Spectator*, XXXVII (1864), 206–207.

14. XVII (Feb. 27, 1864), 254.

15. Henry Tristram, *op. cit.*, p. 40.

16. See Ward, *Life*, II, 8.

17. See Margaret Farrand Thorp, *Charles Kingsley* (Princeton, 1937), p. 160.

18. *Ibid.*, p. 158.

19. *Apologia*, p. 27.

20. *The Life and Works of Charles Kingsley* (19 vols., London, 1901), I, 59 and 73.

21. See Leslie Stephen, "Charles Kingsley," *DNB*, XI, 179, and his *An Agnostic's Apology* (London, 1903), pp. 179–180; James Anthony Froude, *The Nemesis of Faith* (2nd ed., London, 1849), pp. 157–158; and Guy Kendall, *Charles Kingsley and His Ideas* (London, 1947), p. 149.

22. Quoted by Ward, *Life*, II, 11–12, from the *Spectator* of March 26, 1864.

23. Ward, *Life*, II, 13–14.

24. *Apologia*, p. 99.

25. Not on June 25, as Ward says (*Life*, II, 28).

26. Quoted by M. F. Thorp, *Charles Kingsley*, p. 159.

27. *Ibid.*, p. 160.

28. Guy Kendall, *Charles Kingsley and His Ideas*, p. 157.

29. MS *Apologia* Letters, II, No. 7.

30. Ward, *Life*, II, 22.

31. *Ibid.*, pp. 19–20.

32. *Newman: Light in Winter* (New York, 1963), p. 320.

33. MS *Apologia* Letters, I, No. 8.

34. *Ibid.*, I, 61.

35. For Newman's lucid defense of Tract 90 and Maurice's apology, see the *Times* of Feb. 26 and Feb. 27, 1863.

36. MS Pusey Letters, 1860–1864, in the Birmingham Oratory.

37. Meriol Trevor, *Newman: Light in Winter*, p. 317. See also *Charles Kingsley: His Letters and Memories of His Life*. Edited by His Wife (2 vols., London, 1877), II, 191–192, for an indication of the extent and persistence of this feeling among Protestants against the Catholic clergy. It is clear that the Kingsleys never lost it.

38. *Apologia*, p. 36.

39. The letters and newspaper stories alluded to here and below are preserved in a volume called "Personal Attacks, 1834–1883," in the Birmingham Oratory Archives.

40. August 15, 1863, in Ward, *Life*, I, 591. See also *John Henry Newman: Autobiographical Writings*, ed. Henry Tristram (New York, 1957), pp. 84–85, for an 1863 tribute to the dead Whately most revealing when read between the lines.

41. MS *Apologia* Letters, II, No. 43.

42. How deep the hurt was may be seen in the moving letter he wrote her declining the invitation. (Trevor, *Newman: Light in Winter*, pp. 505–506.)

43. Ward, *Life*, I, 526.

44. *Ibid.*, 584–585.

45. See Trevor, *Newman: Light in Winter*, pp. 169–173.

46. See Newman, *On Consulting the Faithful in Matters of Doctrine*, ed. John Coulson (New York, 1961), p. 4.

47. *Ibid.*, p. 2.

48. See his letter to a Catholic friend contemplating the publication of a historical review. Ward, *Life*, I, 571–572.

49. *Ibid.*, 582–583.

50. *Ibid.*, 613.

51. *Ibid.*, 608.

52. *Ibid.*, 541.

53. *Ibid.*, II, 46.

Edward Kelly, S.J.: THE *Apologia*

AND THE ULTRAMONTANES

I*t might* seem strange to discuss Newman's *Apologia* at
any length in connection with the English Catholic group
called the Ultramontanes, since their major representatives
did not appear by name in the first edition of 1864 and
since they were fundamentally, although indiscriminately,
on the same Catholic side that Newman so ably defended
against the charges of the Protestant Charles Kingsley. Yet
biographical research as well as analysis of the *Apologia* itself can reveal significant relationships between this work
and the Ultramontanes. Some of these relationships form
interesting parallels with problems facing the Second Vatican Council and the ecumenically-minded Church of today.

26

The most prominent spokesmen of the English Ultramontanes, who might be briefly described as overly Rome-centered Catholics, are usually listed as: Henry Edward Manning, William George Ward, George Talbot, Frederick William Faber, Bishop Grant, Herbert Vaughan, and to some extent Cardinal Wiseman. Almost every one of these men was at one time a friend or admirer of Newman. Here we cannot analyze all of their individual relations with Newman, but Manning will be our center of focus, for he was the center of English Ultramontanism. It seems clear, for example, that the more Cardinal Wiseman allowed himself to be influenced and guided by Manning, the more ultramontane and the more opposed to Newman he became. He was well disposed toward Manning from his conversion in 1851 onward, and we know now that in 1863 he wrote to Talbot in Rome that he would like Manning to be his successor as Archbishop of Westminster.[1]

Manning and Newman, although often in disagreement, had been fairly good friends ever since Oxford days. In 1857 Newman dedicated his *Sermons Preached on Various Occasions* to Manning, showing his still friendly feelings at this date. From Manning's point of view, according to his own statement, the first thing that shook his confidence in Newman and drove a wedge into their friendship was an article in the *Rambler* of December, 1860, which he erroneously thought had been written or at least supported by Newman.[2] This article attacked Manning's pamphlet on the temporal power of the Pope. Faber, Manning, and Ward were vigorously preaching the necessity of this power and of Catholic loyalty in maintaining it. Manning even thought that a doctrine asserting the Pope's temporal power would be defined.[3] When Sir John Acton, Newman's friend, wrote in the *Rambler* against such views,

Manning warned him that the *Rambler* might be censured from Rome. Newman was annoyed at this authoritarianism and warned Manning that if Wiseman intended to bring up the question of temporal power in the newly formed Academia of the Catholic Religion, he would withdraw his membership. To Wiseman and Manning, then, Newman too appeared disloyal. It was even rumored that he supported Garibaldi.

Closely connected with this issue was that of papal infallibility. Ward's ultramontanism in this area was especially unacceptable to Newman. Ward apparently held that most papal documents, such as encyclicals, were infallible; and one of his famous sayings was: "I should like a new Papal Bull every morning with my *Times* at breakfast." [4] The *Dublin Review* was the organ for such ultramontane views. Manning retained ultimate control over this magazine, but Ward was its editor from 1862. Not only did these men exaggerate the power of the Pope, but they were also despotic in trying to force their own interpretations on Catholics.[5] Those who did not accept their views on papal infallibility were called disloyal and national Catholics.[6]

Newman seems to have first realized Manning's hostile feelings toward him in 1863. In the July number of the *Dublin Review*, Manning, in listing the English Catholic schools of the day, omitted mention of the Oratory School, which Newman had founded a few years earlier. This omission had all the appearances of being calculated, for in the succeeding issue Manning added several schools in a note of correction, but did not add the Oratory School. Certainly the school was being suspiciously watched from London, for as it came out later, Newman was supposedly preparing boys for the Protestant universities with the worldly, literary kind of education traditional to the great English public schools.[7]

To the Ultramontanes, then, Newman was not a full-fledged Catholic; he was still partly Protestant in spirit. The *Rambler* affair and his Oratory School were proof of this. Admittedly, this was a time when the Catholic hierarchy was justly fearful of compromising the purity of Catholicism with Protestant ideas and attitudes. It was a time of religious unrest, and some conversions proved to be very short-lived. It seemed clear that not all the recent Oxford converts had thoroughly abandoned their former religious views. Moreover, the Association for Promoting the Unity of Christendom (A.P.U.C.), founded in 1857 by both Protestants and Catholics and flourishing in the 1860's, was disturbing to Catholic leaders, who thought it was striving for a church unity that was basically the unacceptable unity of three branches. Manning was disappointed with the moderateness with which it was condemned in September, 1864. "I had hoped for more," he complained.[8]

By the time of the *Apologia* Newman knew he was in disfavor in Rome and London. After his article "On Consulting the Faithful in Matters of Doctrine" was delated to Rome, and then when it was suggested that he resign the editorship of the *Rambler*, he decided to remain quiet. "The cause of my not writing from 1859 to 1864," he recorded in later years, "was my failure with the Rambler. I thought I had got into a scrape, and it became me to be silent." [9] But because he was so silent for these five years, much that was pent up and frustratingly self-suppressed in him burst forth in the *Apologia*. Kingsley was not his only target; the Ultramontanes who had kept him silent were also under attack. He had both to correct their false views of his unorthodox

Catholicity and to point out that they themselves were an ultra party and not true representatives of Catholicism.

The wide scope of the *Apologia* no doubt evolved from a complex base of both conscious and unconscious forces. But Father Hugh A. MacDougall has pointed out that Acton's fate with the *Home and Foreign Review* and his suggestions to Newman about writing a more general defense of the Catholic Church quite probably incited Newman to write the final chapter of the *Apologia* as he did. Newman answered Acton: "As to the points you mention, you may be sure I shall go as far as ever I can." [10]

Acton terminated the *Home and Foreign Review* because the Munich Congress at the end of 1863, whose liberal Catholicism he had highly praised in the magazine, was censured by Rome. Newman had objected all along to the serious defects of the *Rambler* and the *Home and Foreign Review* and was always truly respectful of ecclesiastical authority, but he also objected to the authoritarianism which repressed free expression of views on open questions like the relation of science to religion. In the *Apologia* there is a reference to "recent acts of that authority" which have the effect of "tying the hands of a controversialist, such as I should be." [11] This seems to be an allusion to such acts as the Munich Brief.[12]

Although Newman claimed that he would be happy to obey commands not to write on certain questions when these came from the highest authority, he was anything but happy to accept the repression of views demanded by those not in authority, like the writers of the *Dublin Review*. In answering Acton on March 18, 1864, just before writing the *Apologia*, Newman rationalized a little about the good that could come out of the termination of the *Home and Foreign Review*. The English Catholic body would react, he wrote: "I don't think that active and honest minds can remain content under a dull tyranny. It seems impossible to conceive that they can remain quiet under the supremacy of Manning and Ward." [13] In the last chapter of the *Apologia* he repeats this complaint, without mentioning names: the ruling authority "may be accidentally supported by a violent ultra party, which exalts opinions into dogmas, and has it principally at heart to destroy every school of thought but its own." [14] He also reiterates what he had so eloquently proclaimed in the *Development of Christian Doctrine* about the value and even necessity of free and independent religious speculation even when conflict results: "It is necessary for the very life of religion, viewed in its large operations and its history, that the warfare [between authority and private judgment] should be incessantly carried on." [15] The object or effect of the Church's divinely given infallibility, he continues, is "not to enfeeble the freedom or vigour of human thought in religious speculation, but to resist and control its extravagance." [16]

In explaining the centrality of infallibility in Catholic apologetics, Newman seems to have gone out of his way to attack Manning's and Ward's ultramontane views on the subject. But first he carefully affirms that he himself submits to this infallibility, as well as to "those other decisions of the Holy See, theological or not, through the organs which it has itself appointed, which waiving the question of their infallibility, on the lowest ground come to me with a claim to be accepted and obeyed." [17] Having affirmed his belief and loyalty, he then declares the passive and limited nature of this infallibility. The Church's infallible pronouncements are only statements of what is already held in faith by Catholics and are made only after lengthy investigations of the actual faith of Catholics.[18] There will not be many of them;.

scarcely one every morning with the *Times* at breakfast, as Ward wished. Moreover, they are limited to the subjects of faith and morals. So it does not follow "because there is a gift of infallibility in the Catholic Church, that therefore the parties who are in possession of it are in all their proceedings infallible." [19]

Another area in the *Apologia* in which Newman appears to be opposing the Ultramontanes is that centering around things of England: her character and nationality, and the Church of England. He praises them in a number of different contexts, no doubt for various reasons. First of all, Newman was a patriotic Englishman (at times even chauvinistic) who wished to show that there is no conflict between being a good Englishman and being a good Catholic. English Catholics had traditionally been called "un-English." And certainly, rhetorically, Newman was trying to please his English readers. But there were also ecumenical reasons for writing this way. Although he did not join the A.P.U.C., Newman was sympathetic with its groping desire for unity, however vaguely it was expressed. He knew that many Anglicans were offended by the brusque and apparently unsympathetic attitudes of Manning and other Catholic leaders.

One does not have to become Italian or French to be a Catholic, Newman tells his English readers. For now that Pius IX has constituted the Church in England with its own hierarchy (1850), the way is prepared "for our own habits of mind, our own manner of reasoning, our own tastes, and our own virtues, finding a place and thereby a sanctification in the Catholic Church." [20] Faber and Manning had been trying to introduce Italian devotions and ritual into English Catholicism. It is even said that Faber was encouraging Catholics to call the Blessed Virgin

"Mama." But Newman is outspoken about his dislike of
some foreign devotions which "are not suitable for England." [21] On the question of equivocation, he again openly
avows his preference for the English rather than the Italian
"rule of conduct." [22]

The important note on the Anglican Church in the appendix of the *Apologia* was ostensibly written to answer an
accusation made by Kingsley in his pamphlet, but it is also
Newman's outlet for illustrating an ecumenically correct,
Catholic approach to the Church of England. Nothing
could be clearer than his belief that this church is not the
Church of Christ's promises but only a national institution,
a human creation. Still, he maintains that it professes some
religious truths and is a higher form of Christianity than the
various forms of Dissent. As long as Catholicism is so weak
in England, it is even good that it prosper. Newman feared
that if Liberalism triumphed in England, the ordinary approach to the Catholic Church would be destroyed, for
natural religious development, as in his own case, often
proceeds from the lower forms of Christianity to the highest.
"My own idea of a Catholic's fitting attitude towards the
National Church in this its supreme hour," he writes, al-
luding to the great threat of nineteenth-century Liberalism,
"is that of assisting and sustaining it, if it be in our power,
in the interest of dogmatic truth." [23]

The *Apologia* was enthusiastically received by Newman's fellow-Catholics in England; letters of congratulation
poured into the Oratory in Birmingham for the rest of 1864.
Manning wrote a formal note of congratulation to Newman
around May 6, which Newman answered on May 8 thanking
him for his "kind letter." He also wrote Wiseman that "it is
singularly interesting; it is like listening to the voice of one
from the dead." [24] And Bishop Ullathorne claimed that

Manning "said it was the greatest work Newman had done though he thought the two first chapters infra dig." [25] But Manning did not like the last chapter or the note on the Church of England; nor did he like the popularity and influence that Newman, a "minimiser" of Catholic doctrine, gained from the *Apologia.*

Manning must have been initially disappointed that, although many prominent English Catholics were referred to in the kindest terms, he was not once mentioned by name. His friend Ward was included (though not by name) in a group of the second phase of the Oxford Movement whose "cast of mind," Newman writes, was "in no small degree uncongenial to my own." [26] On the other hand, Oakeley, mentioned by name, although part of this same group, is highly praised by Newman. But Oakeley was one of Manning's most fearless opponents in the years preceding the *Apologia,* having supported Errington, whom Manning thought an "English" Catholic. Also, Oakeley and Maguire, Canons of Westminster, were very enthusiastic about the first pamphlets of the *Apologia,* gathering clerical signatures in the diocese for a private address of congratulation and striving to get Newman to answer Kingsley publicly in London. They were apparently opposed by the higher authorities in London, for Maguire warned Newman to refrain in his official reply from "all references to the 'ruling powers.'" [27] That Manning was annoyed with these two men and Newman is clear from his letters to Talbot in Rome: on Feb. 24, 1865, he wrote that Newman was a possibility as Wiseman's successor, "for Oakeley and Dr. Maguire have been literally playing the fool about him in this Kingsley affair." [28]

Nor was Manning happy with the reaction of some Anglicans to the *Apologia.* Newman's expression of kind feelings toward the Church of England naturally pleased

them. In their reviews of the book several Anglican magazines thanked Newman and contrasted his friendly tone
with the hostile attitudes of the Ultramontanes. The reviewer of the *Union Review*, the organ of the A.P.U.C.,
wrote:

It is the difference between a man of large views, broad sympathies, scrupulous candour, and chivalrous generosity, and those
who have done their utmost to divest themselves of every vestige
of individuality, to ignore all their antecedents, to denationalize
their whole habit of mind, and to make themselves into the
mere willing creatures of a great proselytist Propaganda. . . .
He [Newman] has not forgotten either that he was once an
English Churchman.[29]

The London Quarterly Review remarked that Newman's
charitable tone was "so unlike that of many of those who
have taken the same step with himself." Then Manning is
introduced by contrast:

In the tone of his [Newman's] own personal opinions we find
some solution of the enigma why so great a convert has been
treated with such comparative neglect. The bitter sarcasms of
Dr. Manning, his wholesale adoption of every superstition and
his devoted maintenance of the court as well as the cause of
Rome, must be far more to the taste of ordinary Roman con-
troversialists than the tone of one who can speak thus of the
Church of England.[30]

Manning was very sensitive to these devastating comparisons
in the public press. In his old age he bitterly recalled how
"almost every newspaper in England abused and ridiculed
me. My name was never mentioned, but his was brought in
to condemn me; his name was never mentioned, but mine
was brought in to despite me." [31]

But Manning's most effective objection to the *Apologia*,

again expressed to Talbot, who had the ear of the Pope himself, was: "I know that the Anglicans look on the *Apologia* as a plea for remaining as they are." [32] Besides the remarks already mentioned about the religious good accomplished by the Church of England, Newman also expressed the view that conversion to the Catholic Church should be a slow and careful process. In the note on the Church of England he almost begrudgingly concedes that he would be bound under serious sin to receive into the Church any Anglican who after careful thought and prayer and deliberation demanded admittance into it.[33] Newman based this view on his own experience of conversion, in which the most effective human agents were those, like Dr. Russell, who did not "meddle" but indirectly recommended Catholicism to him.[34] Moreover, he knew that a significant number of recent converts had receded to Protestantism, perhaps because of hasty conversions. He was opposed to the quick and splashy manner in which he thought Manning and Faber were making converts in London. From a journal entry made a year previous to the *Apologia* we see that Newman was quite sensitive to a remark made to Ambrose St. John: "Why, he [Newman] has made no converts, as Manning & Faber have." [35] And, finally, he feared that if he unsettled Anglicans, they might become sceptics rather than Catholics.[36]

In defense of Manning, it should be noted that the *Union Review* did interpret Newman's remarks in support of its own concept of church unity, writing that "those who are disposed to make Dr. Newman's conversion a plea for their own, will not find much encouragement here." [37] It claimed that Newman agreed with the Association's objection to individual conversions. *The London Quarterly Review* assured its readers that in the *Apologia*, there is "no condemnation of the Church he has left." Rather, Newman implicitly admits that the Church of England is a "channel of grace," and therefore "he disavows all active efforts at proselyting from her, and limits his action, in this respect, to the extreme case of an 'Anglican who should come to him . . . [saying] I demand admittance into it.' " [38]

Concrete evidence that Manning was disturbed by Newman's treatment of the Church of England in the *Apologia* is found in a pamphlet that he published in November, 1864. He refers to it in a letter to Newman via Oakeley in 1867:

In my letter to Pusey I defended myself from a charge which had been brought against us both. And believing that a passage in the *Apologia* was open to misunderstanding, and knowing that it had been most unfairly used in a Protestant review, I tried to cover both him and myself. [39]

This public letter was the last of three pamphlets to Pusey that he wrote in 1864 on the subject of the Church of England. The stress in these pamphlets is on the absurdity of a church whose ecclesiastical position is ultimately subject not to a divinely guided authority of its own but to the English political system. Manning was converted to Catholicism after the Gorham decision in 1851 and apparently thought that he could encourage other conversions by pointing out the folly of similar political-ecclesiastical disputes of 1864.

The first of these pamphlets was dated March 8,[40] the very time that Kingsley was preparing his pamphlet *What, Then, Does Dr. Newman Mean?* Manning ridicules the Church of England for being impotent to censure the writers of the *Essays and Reviews* who denied the inspiration of Scripture and eternal punishment. The Crown in Council actually reversed a decision to suspend these writers. Manning sharply writes: "My belief is that when the Church of England lost its inherence in the universal Church, the principle of all spiritual and intellectual disease was developed in its blood, and ate into its bone. I do not believe that it is a poisoned vestment which is put upon it from without, but a morbid and manifold disease which is ever reproducing itself from within." [41] He concludes that since this church is not any part of the whole Christian Church, its dissolution is certain and inevitable. Nothing has been discovered to indicate that Newman read this pamphlet, yet his own remarks about Catholics assisting and sustaining the Church of England in the interest of dogmatic truth could conceivably be his answer to it.

Manning's second pamphlet, *The Convocation and the Crown in Council*, dated July 25, contains a reference to the final part of the *Apologia*, which was published six weeks earlier: "I do not recognise the Church of England as that Church [Church of Christ] in any part of it; a belief which, as Dr. Newman has said, nothing but a miracle could reproduce in me." [42] He denies the charge of ill-feeling toward Anglicans or "savage joy" at their discomforts. But at the same time he refuses to grant the privileged position to the Anglican Church that Newman had given it in the *Apologia*. "What I wish to show is, that Anglicanism is identical in principle with all other forms of the Protestant Reformation [essentially rationalistic]." [43] And as if to oppose the impression he thought Newman was giving Anglicans, that they might well remain in the Church of England, Manning concludes this pamphlet with a denial that there is for the present generation the alternative between Anglo-Catholicism and Roman Catholicism. The choice is only between rationalism and Rome.

Next Pusey published the pamphlet *Legal Force of the*

Judgment of the Privy Council, which is at least partly in answer to Manning. Concerning the judgment of the Crown in Council which embarrassed the Anglican Church Pusey writes: "A class of believers joined in the triumph. And while I know that a very earnest body of Roman Catholics rejoice in all the workings of God the Holy Ghost in the Church of England (whatever they think of her), and are saddened in what weakens her who is, in God's hands, the great bulwark against infidelity in this land, others seemed to be in an ecstasy of triumph at this victory of Satan." [44] Here again was implicitly the odious comparison of Newman and Manning which the latter detested so much. And here again was an implicit appeal to Newman's *Apologia* to support the present position of the Church of England. Actually, Newman wrote that it "has hitherto been a serviceable breakwater against doctrinal errors, more fundamental than its own"; [45] Pusey: "the great bulwark against infidelity in this land."

As an answer to both Pusey and Newman, then, Manning responded with his third pamphlet, *The Workings of the Holy Spirit in the Church of England,* published in November, 1864. He allows that the Holy Spirit works *in* various members of the Church of England but is not *of* this Church as such. This, however, could equally be said of the Dissenting churches. Far from being a bulwark against the flood of infidelity in the land, the Church of England is the "mother of all the intellectual and spiritual aberrations which now cover the face of England." [46] This pamphlet can in a sense be called Manning's "apologia," parallel as it is in various ways to Newman's work. In it, for example, we find Manning objecting to the statement that the alternative before Englishmen is Catholicism or atheism. Newman had written that there is "no medium, in true philosophy, between Atheism and Catholicity." [47] And at some length Manning also assures his readers that he loves England. An outspoken friend of Newman, Canon Walker, wrote him about Nov. 14 telling him that Manning had sent him the proofsheets of this pamphlet. He added: "I could not help thinking before I looked at the papers that he meant me to see and perhaps to say whether there was any clash between him and you. I found there was." [48]

Newman knew, of course, that his statements on infallibility and the Church of England might offend the Ultramontanes. In order to have theological protection, he submitted them to some English Jesuit theologians. Whether this was done before or after publication is uncertain, but in any case the Jesuits gave their approval. So did Bishop Ullathorne.[49] Yet within a month after completing the *Apologia* Newman wrote to a friend: "As to my writing more, speaking in confidence, I do not know how to do it. One cannot speak ten words without ten objections being made to each. I am not certain that I shall not have some remarks made on what I have just finished." [50] In the autumn of 1864 Newman was being opposed by the Ultramontanes concerning his establishing a house in Oxford for the care of Catholics in attendance there. Manning went to Rome at the beginning of 1865. Newman's friend Bellasis, also in Rome, wrote on Jan. 23 that he found that Manning was the prime mover in the opposition to Newman's Oxford plan. "Someone or other is undermining Newman at Rome," he adds, "and they say he is not a safe man and they quote some article of his in the *Rambler* and some passages about the Church of England in the *Apologia*." [51] John Hungerford Pollen reported the same opposition to Newman on April 6, writing: "Also to M. [Manning] are attributed strong words against the book [*Apologia*]." [52]

And finally, on Oct. 26, 1865, Newman wrote Father Lockhart that, although Bishop Ullathorne had approved his statements on infallibility, "afterwards an attempt was made at Rome to criticize it—but the Jesuits (I understand) took it up and defended its correctness in all points." [53]

Like Manning, Wiseman wrote Newman praising the *Apologia*.[54] But, again like Manning, he apparently did not like some of Newman's views or some of the reactions to the work. Evidence for this is his treatment of Newman after the *Apologia*. Newman heard that Wiseman was complaining that his letter of congratulation went unanswered. So he wrote the Cardinal on Sept. 28, expressing his regret for causing this displeasure but explaining that he did not see that an answer to congratulation was appropriate. The Cardinal never answered this letter. Then he vigorously opposed Newman throughout the first attempt to establish a house in Oxford shortly after the completion of the *Apologia*. Newman visited Wiseman on Nov. 4, and according to the account of Patterson, the Cardinal treated him rudely.[55]

In conclusion, it may be said that a number of passages in the *Apologia* were aimed at the English Ultramontanes, who in turn became confirmed in their opinion of Newman's anti-Roman and therefore untrustworthy Catholicity. After the *Apologia* Newman is more openly criticized, especially by Manning, Ward, and Talbot, and is strongly opposed in both attempts to establish a house in Oxford. In this post-*Apologia* period we find Ward, who once cried out "Credo in Newmannum," now warning Manning not to be merciful to Newman, who was "exercising a most powerful influence in favour of what is *in fact* (though he doesn't think so):—(1) Disloyalty to the Vicar of Christ, and (2) Worldliness." [56] Talbot, who once proposed to join Newman's Oratory, wildly asserted in 1867 that "Dr. Newman is the most dangerous man in England." [57] Manning had actually given Talbot subjective grounds for this statement, for a year earlier he wrote, as if summing up his objections to the *Apologia:*

Whether he [Newman] knows it or not, he has become the center of those who hold low views about the Holy See, are anti-Roman, cold and silent, to say no more, about the Temporal Power, national, English, critical of Catholic devotions, and always on the lower side. I see no danger of a Cisalpine Club rising again, but I see much danger of an English Catholicism, of which Newman is the highest type. It is the old Anglican, patristic, literary, Oxford tone transplanted into the Church. It takes the line of deprecating exaggerations, foreign devotions, Ultramontanism, anti-national sympathies. In one word, it is worldly Catholicism, and it will have the worldly on its side, and will deceive many.[58]

On his side, Newman continued the battle by writing against both Protestants and Ultramontanes in his important letters to Pusey and the Duke of Norfolk. The *Apologia* definitely won for Newman the good feeling of most English Catholics and many Protestants but it also entangled him in a life-long combat with the English Ultramontanes.

NOTES

1. This letter, dated June 26, 1863, is in the English College, Rome.

2. Edmund Sheridan Purcell, *Life of Cardinal Manning,* 2 vols. (London, 1895), II, 332.

3. *Ibid.,* pp. 152–153.

4. Wilfrid Ward, *The Life of John Henry Cardinal Newman,* 2 vols. (London, 1912), II, 212–213.

5. Edward Healy Thompson, uncle of Francis Thompson the poet, was appointed sub-editor of the *Dublin Review* in 1862. But by 1864 he was prepared to resign his position, for as he wrote to Newman on Dec. 24 of that year, he could not continue to work under Ward's intolerance and editorial interferences. The Jesuit Henry Coleridge, also a writer for the *Dublin*, complained at this same time that Ward was "absolutely intolerant, in his office of Editor, of anything, even on the most open point, that he does not think himself . . . he has frightened away *all* the best Catholic writers—simply by his intolerance and narrow mindedness." These letters are to be found in the archives of the Birmingham Oratory and are used in this writer's unpublished doctoral dissertation, "Cardinal Newman's Unpublished Letters: A Selection from the Year July, 1864 to July, 1865" (Fordham University, 1963), p. 292. Hereafter references to this thesis will be noted simply as Thesis.

6. Ward, II, 83.

7. Purcell, II, 318.

8. *Ibid.*, 284.

9. *John Henry Newman: Autobiographical Writings*, ed. Henry Tristram (London, 1956), p. 272.

10. *The Acton-Newman Relations* (New York, 1962), pp. 91–92.

11. *Apologia Pro Vita Sua: The Two Versions of 1864 and 1865*, ed. Wilfrid Ward (London, 1913), p. 354. Future references to this text will be noted as *Apologia*.

12. Cf. Josef Altholz, *The Liberal Catholic Movement in England* (London, 1962), p. 230.

13. Ward, I, 566.

14. *Apologia*, p. 351.

15. *Ibid.*, p. 344.

16. *Ibid.*, p. 344.

17. *Ibid.*, p. 343.

18. *Ibid.*, pp. 345, 347.

19. *Ibid.*, p. 349.

20. *Ibid.*, p. 359.

21. *Ibid.*, p. 288.

22. *Ibid.*, p. 363. In the first edition Newman wrote "character" rather than "rule of conduct."

23. *Apologia*, p. 396. Cf. Newman's letter to Dean Church of May 2, 1864, where Newman writes: "Don't suppose I shall say one word unkind to the Church of England, at least in my intentions. . . . I simply wrote to state facts, and I can truly say, and never will conceal, that I have no wish at all to do anything against the Establishment while it is a body preaching dogmatic truth, as I think it does at present." Ward, II, 24.

24. Purcell, II, 326n.

25. Thesis, p. 365.

26. *Apologia*, p. 259. Newman is here referring to a precipitant and overly logical cast of mind. Cf. pp. 264–266.

27. Meriol Trevor, *Newman: Light in Winter* (New York, 1963), p. 354.

28. Purcell, II, 206. See also 326n: "The Kingsley affair, about which Canon Oakeley and Dr. Maguire were making fools of themselves."

29. II (Oct., 1864), 486–487.

30. CXVI (Oct., 1864), 290, 291. Similar remarks can be found in the *Christian Remembrancer*, XLVIII (1864), 458–459. Manning complained to Talbot in October, 1864: "Every week, ever since you went, some new evidence of the growth of an English party appears. The Anglicans have already perceived it, and used it in the *Christian Remembrancer*, in the *Union*, and in the *Quarterly*." Purcell, II, 300. Cf. 319, 332.

31. Shane Leslie, *Henry Edward Manning: His Life and Labours* (London, 1921), p. 271.

32. Purcell, II, 323.

33. *Apologia*, p. 397. Bishop Moriarity of Kerry, whom Newman respected, objected that this passage implies that "you

would not go out of your way to bring an Anglican into the Catholic Church, or that you did not very much desire he should come into it." (Thesis, p. 172.) Newman dropped this passage in the second edition of 1865.

34. *Apologia*, p. 287.

35. *Autobiographical Writings*, p. 257.

36. On two different drafts of a reply to Bishop Moriarity's objection (cf. note 33), Newman grumbled that he could have written nothing stronger than he did in the *Apologia:* "I have unsettled to the extent of possible unsettlement. . . . I confess that I think there is *so great* a danger of an Anglican *rather* taking the liberal side than the Catholic, *when* unsettled, that I will not make a great *effort* to unsettle him." Thesis, p. 173.

37. II, 482, 488.

38. CXVI, 291.

39. Purcell, II, 332.

40. *The Crown in Council on the Essays and Reviews*. This as well as the other two pamphlets are found in *England and Christendom* (London, 1867).

41. P. 24.

42. P. 40. Newman wrote (p. 395): ". . . that it [Anglican Church] is something sacred, that it is an oracle of revealed doctrine . . . that it can call itself 'the Bride of the Lamb,' this is the view of it which simply disappeared from my mind on my conversion, and which it would be almost a miracle to reproduce."

43. P. 50.

44. *England and Christendom*, p. 86.

45. *Apologia*, p. 396.

46. P. 115. Newman more gently corrected Pusey's misinterpretation in his letter to Pusey (1865), *Certain Difficulties Felt by Anglicans in Catholic Teaching* (London, 1896), II, 9–11.

47. *Apologia*, p. 291.

48. Thesis, pp. 41–42. On November 18 (1864), Newman wrote in a notebook of philosophical thoughts (soon to be published):

"As to Manning's recent pamphlet, in which he writes against me in my *Apologia* . . . He told Canon Walker it was against me—but there is no need of referring to any testimony, for on the face of it, he wrote to answer the Apologia in those points, or rather to answer his own untrue representations of what I had said in the Apologia. His three charges were: 1. that I had called the Church of England a bulwark of the Catholic Religion or Church.—No, I had called it a *breakwater*. 2. that I had represented that Theism could not be proved by natural reason. I had not, as I have explained above. 3. (I think) that I had said the Catholic proofs were only probabilities. This is the only notice, I believe, he took of my Apologia." Thesis, p. 42.

49. Thesis, p. 366.

50. Ward, II, 43.

51. Trevor, p. 358.

52. Thesis, p. 363.

53. *Ibid.*, p. 88.

54. On July 2, 1864. Miss Trevor has mistakenly written that "not a word came from the Cardinal." (P. 354.) Also, Newman did not send him a copy of the complete work in September, as she states, but in June.

55. Trevor, p. 355.

56. Purcell, II, 309.

57. *Ibid.*, 318.

58. *Ibid.*, 322–323.

Vincent Ferrer Blehl, S.J.: EARLY
CRITICISM OF THE
Apologia

The common impression concerning the press reaction to
the *Apologia* is well represented by Wilfrid Ward's account
in *The Life of John Henry Cardinal Newman* (II, p. 33).
"At that time," he writes, "cultivated opinion was perhaps
better represented by the *Saturday Review* than by any other
journal. And the note struck by the *Saturday* on this subject
when it reviewed the book as a whole, was echoed almost
universally." The following is the account of the *Saturday*
as quoted by Ward:

A loose and off-hand, and, we may venture to add, an un-
justifiable imputation, cast on Dr. Newman by a popular writer,

47

more remarkable for vigorous writing than vigorous thought, has produced one of the most interesting works of the present literary age. Dr. Newman is one of the finest masters of language, his logical powers are almost unequalled, and, in one way or other, he has influenced the course of English thought more perhaps than any of his contemporaries. If we add to this the peculiar circumstances of his reappearance in print, the sort of mystery in which, if he has not enveloped himself, he has been shrouded of late years, the natural curiosity which has been felt as to the results on such a mind of the recent progress of controversy and speculation and the lower interest which always attaches to autobiographies and confessions and personal reminiscences, we find an aggregate of unusual sources of interest in such a publication.

The *Times,* Ward continues, though not so enthusiastic as the *Saturday Review* or the *Spectator,* did not fall far behind.

In saying that the note struck by the *Saturday Review* was echoed almost universally, Ward is misleading, for he gives the impression that the tone of the *Saturday Review* represented the type of response given by most periodicals of the day. A careful scrutiny of the fifty or sixty reviews of the *Apologia* reveals that the reaction was not at all uniform but exceedingly complex, subtle, and nuanced. Those who conceded that Newman's sincerity had been vindicated generally did not agree with his doctrinal views. Some paid a polite tribute to his honesty as a thinker and a theologian but proceeded to qualify that judgment, in some instances, to such an extent that one finds it difficult to understand how the reviewer could have been fully honest in asserting his belief in Newman's sincerity. There were those who straightforwardly affirmed that Newman was sincere, but who with confident self-assurance declared that he was deluded, deranged, a skeptic, emotionally unbalanced, over-imaginative or in need of the external support and security that only the Catholic Church could give. His conversion to Catholicism, however irrational, was said to be perfectly understandable in psychological terms. Others, though a minority, thought that Newman had not vindicated himself against Kingsley's charge. Still others thought that however sincere Newman might be as an individual, he had nonetheless joined a church which by common agreement was shifty, cunning, and unsolicitous for truth. This viewpoint summarizes the problem that confronted nearly every reviewer in greater or less degree. If Newman were sincere and if he had a commanding intellect, how was one to "explain" his conversion to Catholicism? Some ignored the *Apologia* almost entirely, using it simply as a springboard to discuss controversial religious questions brought forward by the contents of the book. It is surprising how relatively little space, in any of the reviews, is given to the style and literary quality of the work. Again, the reviewers who recognized its literary values represented every shade of confessional commitment as well as a wide variety of attitudes toward Newman. Relatively few reviewers were sufficiently detached to combine unqualified acknowledgment of Newman's sincerity with a sympathetic understanding of his successive religious commitments, and a recognition of the outstanding literary quality of his work.

The most generous reviews conceded that the differences between Newman and themselves were differences such as any honest intellect could have. Such were the reviews mentioned by Ward: the *Saturday Review*, the *Spectator* and the *Times*. Others were the *Inquirer*, the *Churchman*, the *Examiner*, *Blackwood's Edinburgh*, the *Guardian*, the *Quarterly Review*, the *Union Review*, the *Church Review*, the

Press, and *John Bull. Blackwood's Edinburgh* is typical of their response. It concludes: "Dr. Newman is wrong, because his principles are indefensible *ab initio,* however perfectly they agree one with another. His error, however, is that of a great mind, which like vaulting ambition, had 'overleaped its sell, and fallen on the other side.' " [1] The *Inquirer* was equally qualified but no less generous. "However much we may differ from Dr. Newman, however far we may be from feeling the full force of many of his positions, we can see how fully *he* feels them, and respect the perfect integrity of his action at every point of his career." [2]

This response is understandable to a degree in light of the habitual attitudes of these papers or of their relationship with Newman. The *Union Review* and the *Church Review* represented that section of the Anglican Church which was most given to the imitation of Roman Catholic ceremonies; they were interested also in the ultimate reunion of the Anglican and Roman Churches. The *Churchman,* also of High Church persuasion, treated Newman favorably as a person, while pointing out what it considered his theological errors. By a careful selection of individual passages, it stressed "Newman's great sorrow at leaving the Anglican Church."

The *Church and State Review* typifies the general tone of Anglican reviews in its statement: "no one in his sound senses can doubt that Dr. Newman has spent a life of tolerable length in an attempt to find out the truth; and that he has, at all and every cost, simply adhered to that which has seemed to him to be the truth." Like that in *Churchman,* this review betrays a touch of nostalgia at what it considered his somewhat tragic defection from the Anglican fold:

It is enough for us to avow, which we do most frankly, that from first to last his conduct has been that of an honest and truth-loving man, and that we only regret, in common with thousands and tens of thousands of our and his fellow-country-men, to see him in this advanced period of his life condemned to eke out his livelihood as a teacher of small boys in a private school at Edgbaston, instead of influencing society at large by his masterly pen and his resistless eloquence, as he might have done if he had remained at Oxford.[3]

It has been suggested, probably most rightly, that the favorable reception of the *Apologia* on the part of the Anglican press was in part due to the kind way in which Newman dealt with his former friends and enemies alike.

Of the non-religious magazines, the *Spectator* was edited by Hutton, who disagreed with Newman's religious convictions but admired his penetrating intellect and his saintly qualities. Moreover Hutton corresponded with Newman during the period between the early stages of the controversy with Kingsley and the appearance of the *Apologia*.[4] R. W. Church, who wrote the review in the *Guardian*, had, on the occasion of Kingsley's attack, re-established his friendship with Newman on an active basis.

The *Saturday Review*, which avoided theological controversy and discussed religious questions only so far as they related to the general social interest of the nation, "was an organ of moderation and toleration." [5] The *Examiner* (religiously neutral), however much it disagreed with Newman on rational grounds, did not wish to see him attacked by fallacious reasoning. Its review is more an attack on Kingsley than a review of the *Apologia*. *Blackwood's* (religiously neutral) also devoted a good deal of its article to attacking Kingsley, as did the *Press* (strong anti-Roman Catholic and Low Church bias), which called the *Apologia* "perfectly honest and courageous" but insisted that it represented the views of a unique individual, who was unlikely to be imitated by the run-of-the-mill reader of their periodical.[6]

The *Quarterly Review* (High Church bias), taking a stand similar to that of the *Press*, magisterially proclaimed that the causes of Newman's defection were the peculiarities of the individual and that persons governed by argument and reason rather than by impulse and feeling would be influenced neither by the conversion of Newman nor by the account of the mental processes through which he came to adopt the Roman Catholic faith. It issued a warning, one more specific than that of the *Press*, to unwary readers who might unwittingly be influenced by the wily Newman: "never is he more a controversialist than when he avoids controversy. There is more force in the burning words he drops, impregnated with the fire of his own inner life, than in the closest of his studied arguments." [7] It enumerated and cautioned against what it considered carefully concealed controversial passages in the work.

The generosity of these reviews was surpassed however by the weekly paper *John Bull* (favorable to High Church principles), which described the *Apologia* as a "work that may assuredly be ranked as a contribution of permanent importance to the literature of the Christian Church." With delightful bluntness, it described Newman as "too essentially a logician, we suspect, to rest satisfied with that practical compromise which is after all the predominant characteristic of the Church of England. . . . We are inclined to think that Dr. Newman's present position is the one best calculated to satisfy his own spiritual and intellectual requirements and that he was not a man who could have permanently rested in our Church." [8]

While all these reviews disagreed with Newman in one way or another, by and large they acknowledged his honesty and sincerity. Most of them judged that he had vindicated himself against the accusations of Kingsley, though they could not approve of his conversion to Catholicism, nor even, in some instances, of his theological views as an Anglican.

At the other end of the spectrum were the completely unfavorable reviews. The *Athenaeum* (religiously neutral), which supported Kingsley in its early reviews of the controversy, continued to do so in its review of the *Apologia*. The reviewer selected passages that offered scope for sharp remarks. For example, in quoting Newman's statement that he was never able to make out what he meant by saying he had not sinned against light, the reviewer commented: "we fancy many persons will be able to join in that exclamation." [9] The *British Quarterly Review* (Congregational and Baptist) merely thought Kingsley guilty of an unfortunate journalistic slip:

If, instead of saying 'Father Newman informs us that,' etc., he had written, 'Father Newman says,' 'or seems to say, that,' etc., all would have been safe. His antagonist, who has pounced on the above three lines with the animus of a vulture, would not in that case have gained the vantage ground which he has used with such resolute animosity against him. Dr. Newman is a wary, subtle, and far-seeing antagonist on all questions of this nature; but, unconsciously to himself, he has supplied, if not a full vindication of the language of Professor Kingsley, certainly a very natural, and almost sufficient, excuse for the use of it.[10]

The *Boston Review* (Congregational) compared Newman's triumph in clearing himself of false representation with the dubious success of Judas: "His success is, to our mind, much of a piece with him who, having gone out and hanged himself, burst asunder in the midst." [11] The *Christian Observer* (Low Church) thought the whole mental portraiture of the *Apologia* betrayed "an utter want of reverence of truth for the truth's sake." After tracing the history of Newman's opinions, rather unsympathetically, the reviewer concludes: "and how then, after all, are these suspicions removed? At what price has he gained a right to be acquitted of direct conscious duplicity and dishonesty? At the price of revealing a union of presumptuous self-confidence, diseased fancy, and mental blindness, which would hardly have been credited except from his own confession." [12]

The reviews that fall between these two extremes are difficult to categorize. The *Clerical Journal* (Church of England weekly), for example, opens with a tribute. Like the confessions of J. J. Rousseau and St. Augustine, the *Apologia* is said "to be the utterance of the true movements and feelings of his own experience." "Had we discovered the marks of that guile which so many think inseparable from Roman Catholics, or of that double-faced tendency which Professor Kingsley insinuates, such an apology might have interested us as a work of fiction, and that would have been all." But this equitable estimate is successively qualified in the course of the review, by such remarks as "it appears to us to be a pitiable situation in which a man is placed when by exalting reason too much he mars his happiness, and can only restore himself to content by abnegating that reason altogether." Again, "Dr. Newman, in this apology, displays the same ignorance of the nature of a true logical inference, as has been the cause of all his previous eccentricities." Newman, though acknowledged to be "a man of genius," is nevertheless in the final analysis an idiot:

While, therefore, we give Dr. Newman all credit for sincerity, and do not wish to rob him of any mental peace which may be genuine and well-founded, we are compelled to regard him as under hallucinations. . . . It is not necessary to be insane, in the legal sense, in order to have the principle of insanity active within us. . . . We may give a man entire credit for being sincere, without conceding that his opinions are true, of course; and this is precisely how we feel in regard to Dr. Newman. He says he believes such and such things, and we feel sure he does . . . and such *faith* should, we think, rather be called an unreasoning credulity.[13]

The *Evangelical Witness* opened its review with a candid, though qualified, admission that Newman "has written out a full history of his religious opinions with a frankness that inspires the conviction that it is genuine as far as it goes." The qualifying phrase "as far it goes" can hardly be considered unfavorable in the summary of the *Apologia* it precedes. But the sudden shift in the middle of the last paragraph of the review raises the question, how sincere is the reviewer's earlier, apparently favorable, judgment of Newman's honesty? "It is brimful of the subtlest thought, the self-revelation of a marvellous intellect grappling with the greatest problems of our human life and destiny." "But"—and here comes the reversal—

it is painful and revolting in its details—the narrative of the gradual darkening of a man's soul to the light, the gradual darkening of his faculties to the holiness of truth; and the miserable boast runs underneath that their destruction is for the interests of God's kingdom. Nor by his own showing does it leave Dr. Newman better; it leaves him ten times worse than when Mr. Kingsley accused him in his haste of teaching that 'cunning is the weapon which Heaven has given to the saints wherewith to withstand the brute male force of the wicked world.' [14]

The cunning and wily Newman could have taken a cue from the less than candid reviewer of the *Evangelical Witness*.

But if an award could be presented for what might be

called the battledore and shuttlecock approach to the problem of Newman's sincerity, it would undoubtedly be given to *Fraser's Magazine* (Broad Church bias), which claimed that though Newman might be honest as a person, his system was dishonest. How Newman's powerful intellect could be honest while embracing a totally dishonest system occupies the ingenuity of the reviewer for the remainder of his article. He concedes, for example, that it is difficult to associate the notion of dishonesty in any form with Newman. Furthermore, he praises the *Apologia* as "a winning, and in some ways, a touching book. It is full of courage and straight-forwardness; every word that the author says of himself and his opinions bears upon it the stamp of truth." But then the tone is somewhat altered: "Almost all of us, he seems to think, are to be damned to all eternity; but with amiable inconsistency he wishes for our good opinion. He would like us to think kindly of him in hell fire." And somewhat later on: ". . . high as Dr. Newman's personal character is, we cannot read this book without feeling that his theology is dangerous sophistry, calculated to serve no other purpose than that of drugging the minds of men who care more for peace of mind than for truth, and whose *ultima ratio* is found not in their reason, but in their fears or their fancies."

The reviewer shifts back and forth from approval to disapproval, but Newman gradually emerges as a cunning sophist. Newman craftily insinuates "by throwing the necessary dash of pathetic obscurity into his argument at the right moment, by saying that an argument does not 'warm or enlighten' him, when he ought to say roundly whether he believes in it or not." Newman seems to the reviewer like "a man who, having been infatuated by a woman neither young, lovely, nor virtuous, marries her at the expense of destroying all his prospects in life, and of throwing up all his connexions, and who then exhausts every resource of his mind in proving that she combines, in ideal perfection, eternal youth, perfect beauty, and every moral and mental grace which could adorn such a person." In the final analysis, "surely it is neither unjust nor uncharitable to say of such a man that he does not care for truth as truth; that he builds castles in the air and not on the ground; and that the general tendency of his writings and speculations is unfavourable to honesty in its widest sense." [15]

Several magazines published pieces that were not so much reviews of the *Apologia* as articles occasioned by the *Apologia*. Their real intent was either to refute Newman's religious positions or to affirm those of the particular periodical. Such were the reviews in the *British and Foreign Evangelical Review*, the second article in the *Evangelical Christendom*, the *Christian Remembrancer* (High Church), the *Ecclesiastic* (High Church), and the *Eclectic Review* (Congregationalist and Baptist), to name but a few. The *Westminster Review*, for example, used the *Apologia* to advocate a liberal, rationalistic attitude towards religion, a position entirely foreign to Newman. The reviewer argued that it was illogical for Protestants to attack Newman for taking refuge in the authority of Rome since they take refuge in the external authority of the Bible. "Men need depend neither on the Bible nor on the Pope." The alternative to the principle of authority is not unbelief but the principle of freedom in which God talks with man " 'as a man talketh with his friend.' " [16]

This sort of review generally acknowledges Newman's sincerity, but then introduces such qualifications that the image of a completely sincere individual becomes considerably blurred in the course of the review. The *Theological*

Review (Unitarian), after paying tribute to Newman's personal sincerity and veracity, asserts that the *Apologia* suffers from the defects of all biographies: it presents only one side and even then it is possible to detect the points at which Newman "must have appeared something less than candid to the common judgment of mankind." [17] Several pages later the reviewer judges that Newman's zeal for the tractarian movement showed itself "on one side in a fierce intolerance, on the other in a carelessness as to the methods of action, the confession of which lends some justification to Mr. Kingsley's indictment." [18] Likewise, the *British and Foreign Evangelical Review*, while conceding that no one would be disposed thereafter to make further imputations on Newman's personal honesty, nonetheless affirms that Newman's mind was so subtle that it led him into courses that looked dishonest. It is furthermore alleged that neither pure indignation nor pure simplicity lay at the bottom of the autobiography, but rather that Newman used the occasion to sway men's minds on questions far more important than those that respect the consistency and integrity of either member of the controversy. Newman had done the only thing he could do by accepting the doctrines of the Roman Church. "But this is the history of a man led by his tendencies, his circumstances, his temptations in a word, to renounce as unsatisfying rational methods of assurance, and to seek certainty, or 'certitude,' by others of his own contrivance, embodying a private method of providential gravitation, as it were, toward the true and the divine." [19] Characteristic of this ambivalent attitude on the part of those reviews that used the *Apologia* as a springboard for attacks upon Newman's religious beliefs is the summary statement of the *Ecclesiastic* (High Church): "Truthfully as the story is told, it reveals the more distinctly, by reason of the speaker's unconsciousness, the latent disease which made him retire from the battle-field into a land of spiritual exile." [20]

The conclusion to be drawn from these reviews is that Newman indeed has vindicated his honesty but at what a price! He fails to leave "the impression of a commanding intellect." [21] In the Church of Rome he has found the "rest of the captive and of the slave," having preferred his "subjective impression" of Rome "to the objective reality." [22] He has destroyed his readers' illusions, for now we see "he was at best but a blind leader of the blind," led by imagination rather than by reason and therefore, "viewed as an intellectual confession," the *Apologia* "is a story of weakness, not of strength." [23] "His great intellect is enchained not only to a deep religious sentiment, but to a superstitious imagination. He is essentially a visionary, whose faith would rise in the exact ratio of the improbable, who would think it part of the excellency of faith to do violence to reason." [24] Finally, "in some points" he is "intellectually weak almost to imbecility." [25]

Although most reviewers were too preoccupied with the religious question to take account of the literary quality of the work, at least ten recognized the *Apologia* as a work of extraordinary value, to be ranked among the great works of literature. Their comments, however, are usually quite brief. The reviewers in the *Press*, the *Patriot*, and the *Saturday Review*, praised the *Apologia* as a psychological portrait. Said the *Patriot*: "As a revelation of character the 'Apologia' stands almost alone, not only in the peculiar circumstances which have to be explained, but in the stern, judicial, unfaltering, and unfearing self-analysis of it. While it reminds us of Augustine's confessions, it is a far deeper revelation, and a far greater moral achievement than they." [26] The portraiture was also praised for its vividness as well as its depth, one reviewer noting the effect on the reader of "the intense moral solitude of his soul, over and above the insulated integrity of his intellect." [27]

The *American Quarterly Church Review*, which saw in the *Apologia* a perfect unity of design and purpose, admired the way in which the narrative was arranged for dramatic effect.[28] Others caught the simplicity of tone, the artlessness and naturalness of its language, and the clearness of statement "in which all his facts sparkle brightly like the stars in a cloudless sky." [29] The manliness of tone and the felicity of its statement did not escape the reviewer in the *Patriot*, who proclaimed that "one of the most remarkable books of this, or any other age, has been added to our literature—a book which, in after generations, will be read with as much interest as it is now." [30] And finally, "as an authentic contribution to the history of a most important and critical episode in the English Church, and as a personal revelation of immense psychological interest," the *Press* maintained that "the 'Apologia' will always remain a precious and unique composition." [31]

NOTES

1. *Blackwood's Edinburgh Magazine*, XCVI (Sept. 1864), 308.

2. *Inquirer*, June 18, 1864.

3. The *Church and State Review*, Aug. 1, 1864.

4. This no doubt explains why the tone of the review of June 4, 1864 is much softer than that of the previous review of the Correspondence, on February 20, 1864, in which the reviewer had said "one of the greatest secrets of Dr. Newman's wonderful power is an intellectual basis for his mind of that peculiar hardness tending to cruelty which most easily allies itself with

a keen intellectual sense of the supernatural," and "we believe Dr. Newman's writings show . . . that a layer of very fine, and delicate, and generous sympathies overlying a deep and imperturbable scorn . . . is a still deeper source of knowledge of human nature [than sympathy]," and "the sarcasm of the theological imagination . . . is the ground-work of Dr. Newman's greatest literary power."

5. Merle Mowbray Bevington, *The Saturday Review, 1855–1868. Representative Educated Opinion in Victorian England* (New York, 1941), p. 77. I wish to acknowledge the assistance of my students in Seminar 575, Sister M. Therese Waldmann, S.S.J., Francis Gillen, and Sister Mary James, O.P., in determining the religious bias of the various periodicals and magazines cited.

6. ". . . We repeat, then, that the whole 'Apologia' is the history of the feelings of an individual, and that no one is likely to receive from it any fresh bias towards Rome who had not gone four-fifths of the way by himself already. In other words, to be affected as Newman was, a man must be a second Newman. As an authentic contribution to the history of a most important and critical episode in the English Church, and as a personal revelation of immense psychological interest, the 'Apologia' will always remain a precious and unique composition. As an active agent in determining men's minds either one way or the other, we hold it of small account." The *Press*, July 16, 1864.

7. The *Quarterly Review* (London). I cite the American edition called *London Quarterly Review*, CXVI (Oct. 1864), 292. This is not to be confused with *London Quarterly Review*, which was Methodist.

8. *John Bull*, July 23, 1864.

9. *Athenaeum*, May 21, 1864.

10. The *British Quarterly Review*, XL (July 1, 1864), 103.

11. The *Boston Review*, V (Jan. 1865), 33.

12. The *Christian Observer*, LXIII (Sept. 1864), 672, 683.

13. The *Clerical Journal*, July 7, 1864.

14. The *Evangelical Witness and Presbyterian Review*, III (Sept. 1864), 228–229.

15. *Fraser's Magazine*, LXX (Sept. 1864), 266, 276, 278.

16. The *Westminster Review* (American edition), LXXXII (Oct. 1864), 176, 177.

17. The *Theological Review*, I (July 1864), 313.

18. *Ibid.*, 319.

19. The *British and Foreign Evangelical Review*, XIII (Oct. 1864), 803.

20. *Ecclesiastic*, XXVI (July 1864), 310.

21. *North British Review*, XLI (Aug. 1864), 104.

22. *Evangelical Christendom*, XVIII, New Series (Sept. 1864), 428, (Oct. 1864), 482.

23. *London Review*, June 25, 1864.

24. The *Patriot*, July 21, 1864.

25. *Weekly Review*, June 25, 1864.

26. The *Patriot*, July 21, 1864. The *Union Review*, II (1864), 481, spoke in the same accents: "Since the *Confessions* of S. Augustine were given to the world, we doubt if any autobiography has appeared of such thrilling interest as the present, both from the character and genius of the writer, and from the graphic power and minuteness with which he has traced the progress of his own mind through speculations of the deepest moment, and during an eventful period. . . ."

27. "*Apologia Pro Vitâ*" *Ecclesiae Anglicanae*, a pamphlet attributed to Dr. Irons, which appeared first in a slightly shortened form in the *Literary Churchman*, July 2, 1864.

28. The *American Quarterly Church Review*, XVII (April 1865), 5. The *London Quarterly Review*, (i.e., American edition of the *Quarterly Review* [London]), CXVI (Oct. 1864), 274, also commented on its dramatic quality: "As an autobiography, in the highest sense of that word, as the portraiture, that is,

and record of what the man was, irrespective of those common accidents of humanity which too often load the biographer's pages, it is eminently dramatic."

29. The *Press*, June 11, 1864.

30. The *Patriot*, July 21, 1864. Similarly the reviewer in the *Christian Remembrancer*, XLVIII (July 1864), 162, praised "its felicity of arrangement, its lucid style, its freshness and humour . . . its manliness of tone."

31. The *Press*, July 16, 1864. *John Bull*, July 23, 1864, in a similar vein called it "a work that may assuredly be ranked as a contribution of permanent importance to the literature of the Christian Church."

William E. Buckler: THE *Apologia*

AS HUMAN EXPERIENCE

I am not here today because I am a Newman specialist, and I'm certainly not a theologian. I am here merely as a professor with a point of view. In *Arts and Sciences,* a magazine "maintained by New York University as a mirror for the intellectual life of the institution in the area of the liberal arts and pure sciences . . . ," I published an article entitled "A Dual Quest: The Victorian Search for Identity and Authority" [1]—an article which, incidentally, had first been given as a lecture here at Fordham University. In that article, I said that "a critical method well calculated to take significant measure of Victorian literature in its true length and breadth must recognize in Victorian literature a literature not mainly of argument but of experience." In partial support of that thesis, I went on to say the following:

64

In Memoriam, like the *Apologia*, is one of the hallmarks of Victorianism—not because it reviews in a searching way representative ideas and arguments, but because it relates those ideas and arguments to personality. In both *In Memoriam* and the *Apologia* are focussed the Victorian search for identity and authority on terms which were not possible before 1830 or after, say, 1870. They are both designedly "unreasonable" documents, set against the whole tide of English rationalism. In them, Tennyson and Newman evolve only one argument: this is an honest portrait of an honest man whose conclusions one must accept not as abstractly true or false, but as personally so. In Tennyson's poem, we have a created *persona*: the "I" of *In Memoriam* is an imaginary poet, not Alfred Tennyson. *In Memoriam* is, as I see it, in no *essential* way autobiographical, though it loosely employs an autobiographical framework. Even the *Apologia*, though clearly and explicitly autobiographical, also has its *persona*, its "not me," which the author is pursuing. Newman's "Preface" of 1865 gives us an insight into this quality:

Yes, I said to myself, his very question is about my meaning; 'What does Dr. Newman mean?' It pointed in the very same direction as that into which my musings had turned me already. He asks what I mean; not about my words, not about my arguments, not about my actions, as his ultimate point, but about the living intelligence, by which I write, and argue, and act. He asks about my Mind and its Beliefs and its sentiments; and he shall be answered. . . .

Elsewhere in the same article I also have this to say of Newman:

John Henry Newman's is perhaps the best known religious pilgrimage of modern times. His clear, subtle, sensitive, critical intelligence worked its painful way among the shams and shadows of the "new philosophy." Driven by a nature which was innately irrational, he yet sought a deeply personalized solution to the modern dilemma, which the facts of history and his own reason, honestly employed, would sustain. Newman was himself a supremely educated man. Yet *The Idea of a University* is, ultimately, a devastating indictment of the educated man; and the "gentleman" which is education's best end product is a figure with which no man of truly imaginative vision would allow himself willingly to be identified. It is Newman's basic thesis that "a cultured intellect, a delicate taste, a candid, equitable, dispassionate mind, a noble and courteous bearing in the conduct of life" are excellent things in themselves, but that, equally, they are not what they are not. They are not sanctity, for example, nor virtue, nor even conscientiousness. "Quarry the granite rock with razors, or moor the vessel with a thread of silk; then may you hope with such keen and delicate instruments as human knowledge and human reason to contend against those giants, the passion and the pride of man." Newman felt that the springs of action lay, not in knowledge, but in belief: "Life is for action. If we insist on proofs for everything, we shall never come to action: to act you must assume, and that assumption is faith." Newman's discountenancing of that aspect of the Renaissance which we call the Reformation was, then, inevitable; and it is not surprising that he laid his heart on the medieval altars of Rome, or that, where his heart lay, there he let his mind lie also.

The context in which these remarks were made was, of course, very different from that of a symposium devoted entirely to the *Apologia*. But I find myself willing to defend their general validity, and the point of view that they express will control much of what I say today. I have no apologies to make for the high value that I personally set upon Newman: without any of Mr. Kingsley's sarcasm, I consider him "the most acute man of his generation." But as a professor of Victorian literature, I find it necessary to remind myself regularly of remarks like Walter Houghton's: "No biography so concrete and human as the *Apologia* was ever so difficult to read. Most readers find much of it obscure, oblique, and indigestible." [2] The problem of the professor, then, is one of method: how can he prepare a generation of students who read on the run and to whom religious controversy is positively repugnant to read the *Apologia* with that sympathetic understanding which constitutes the essential condition for a significant literary experience? How can he keep the *Apologia* from being lost as literature?

In the first place, he should condition his students' reaction to the style of the *Apologia*. They will not find there long, elaborate sentences, marvelous in their workmanship; nor the customary wealth of literary and historical allusion; nor the calm flow of carefully wrought sentences which swell into great emotional climaxes. But the style of the *Apologia* is none the less apposite; and the speed with which it was written, if one recalls the pain with which Newman habitually wrote, becomes almost a dimension of its character. Students need to be informed of certain external and internal conditions which deeply affected Newman when he sat down to write and which provide, from one angle of vision, an acceptable explanation for his having been "found more than once with his head in his hands, crying like a child," not only "over the sadness of the memories which his task recalled," but also over the herculean trial to which he had subjected himself. Here I would like to catalogue and illustrate some of these conditions:

(a) *His early compulsion to write:*

The unpleasant style in which it is written arises from my habit, from a boy, *to compose.* I seldom wrote anything without an eye to style, and since my taste was bad my style was bad. I wrote in style as another might write in verse, or sing instead of speaking, or dance instead of walking. [3]

(b) The importance of "occasions":

What I have written has been for the most part what may be called official, works done in some office I held or engagement I had made—all my Sermons are such, my Lectures on the Prophetical Office, on Justification, my Essays in the *British Critic*, and translation of St. Athanasius—or has been from some especial call, or invitation, or necessity, or emergency, as my Arians, Anglican Difficulties, "Apologia" or Tales. The Essay on Assent is nearly the only exception. And I *cannot* write without such a *stimulus*. I feel myself going out of the way, or impertinent, and I write neither with spirit nor with point.[4]

(c) His perfectionist approach to writing:

I write, I write again: I write a third time in the course of six months. Then I take the third: I literally fill the paper with corrections, so that another person could not read it. I then write it out fair for the printer. I put it by; I take it up: I begin to correct again: it will not do. Alterations multiply, pages are re-written, little lines sneak in and crawl about. The whole page is disfigured; I write again; I cannot count how many times this process is repeated.[5]

(d) His feelings of pain in the act of writing:

It is one of my sayings, (so continually do I feel it) that the composition of a volume is like gestation and child-birth. I do not think that I ever thought out a question, or wrote my thoughts, without great pain, pain reaching to the body as well as to the mind. It has made me feel practically, that labour *in sudore vultus sui*, is the lot of man, and that ignorance is truly one of his four wounds. It has been emphatically *a penance*; and in consequence I have hardly written anything, unless I was *called* to do it, e.g., I had to provide a sermon weekly for the pulpit &c. I recollect a friend asked me, soon after writing my volume on Justification, whether it was not interesting to write, and my answer was to the effect that "it was the painful relieving of an irritation," as a man might go to a dentist, not for "keen and constant pleasure," but with the mingled satisfaction and distress of being rid of pain *by* pain. When I wrote the Arians six years earlier, I was so exhausted at length, that for some days as it approached finishing, I could scarce keep from fainting.[6]

(e) *His desire to have spiritual children:*

The thought keeps pressing on me, while I write this, what am I writing it for? For myself, I may look at it once or twice in my life, and what sympathy is there in *my* looking at it? Whom have I, whom can I have, who would take an interest in it? . . . I willingly give up the possession of that sympathy [which a wife gives], which I feel is not, cannot be, granted to me.— Yet, not the less I feel the need of it. Who will care to be told such details as I have put down above? Shall I ever have in my old age spiritual children who will take an interest such as a wife does? [7]

(f) *His sense of the individuality and personality of style:*

It is not some production or result, attained by the partnership of several persons, or by machinery, or by any natural process, but in its very idea it proceeds, and must proceed, from some one given individual. Two persons cannot be the authors of the sounds which strike our ear; and, as they cannot be speaking one and the same speech, neither can they be writing one and the same lecture or discourse,—which must certainly belong to some one person or other, and is the expression of that one person's ideas and feelings,—ideas and feelings personal to himself, though others may have parallel and similar ones,—proper to himself, in the same sense as his voice, his air, his countenance, his carriage, and his action, are personal. . . . His thought and feeling are personal, and so his language is personal.[8]

Although the *Apologia* would hardly be cited as an example of the emotive and incantatory Newman, it does project at least three of his voices: the gladiatorial challenge of Part I; the subdued plainspeaking, punctuated with pathos and delicacy, of Parts III–VI; the careful documentation and analysis of the Appendix. It is perhaps worth asserting that there are no tears in Part I of the *Apologia*: there Newman's agony is not of the cloister but of the arena; there, with power and passion and precision, he so drives his antagonist before him that one must marvel at the bold directness of his style of combat. The Newman of Mr. Kingsley's report—"in weak health, . . . [wishing] for peace and quiet, and . . . averse to controversy" [9]—has certainly had a most miraculous recovery!

In the second place, students should be encouraged to read the *Apologia* not only as the autobiography of an individual man, but also as a spiritual odyssey, even as a spiritual romance. It is misleading, I think, to approach Newman as a man who went from Evangelicalism to Liberalism to a defined Anglicanism to Roman Catholicism. It is true that he did pass through various stages which can legitimately be so named. No doubt the quality of Newman's Catholicism was affected by his youthful Evangelicalism; and the Newman of 1816 lived on in the Newman of 1845. But to the average reader, these designations of religious parties are more or less foreign terms, perhaps somewhat prejudicial in themselves. It is better, I think, to look upon these various stages as symbolic resting-places in Newman's pilgrimage— call it psychological, intellectual, spiritual, or philosophical as you will—from individualism to institutionalism, from self-regarding emotionalism to self-abnegating authoritarianism. Thus the *Apologia* is more essentially the record of a flight *from* Liberalism than of a flight *to* Roman Catholicism. Newman looked upon the Liberals as the whole "educated lay world," and, as he said at the time of receiving the cardinalate, his life-work had been the fight against Lib-

eralism. Liberalism, he felt, was the halfway house to spiritual, philosophical, moral, and social chaos. Built on the
unstable foundation of reason, which history showed had
led to error more frequently than to truth, it denied real
spirituality and reduced philosophy to complete relativism,
morality to social custom, and social justice to expendiency.
He departed, therefore, in search of the certainty that his
nature demanded. Like Carlyle, he held a sacramental view
of the universe, but unlike Carlyle, he could not be satisfied with anything so abstract as a "transcendental idea." His
imagination needed a concrete realization of that idea, a
realization that was old enough and universal enough to
have earned independence of time and place. This he felt
he found in Rome.

Newman was a spokesman not only for Roman Catholics, but also, in many respects, for those of his contemporaries who, against the rising tide of Liberalism, would hold
to traditional Christianity. Many orthodox believers sought
to combat Liberalism through vehement reiteration of traditional arguments or to flee from it into ritualism. Newman
entered into the psychology of his age and offered not the
ever-disputable evidences but the indisputable fact of his
own acceptance of them.

Newman is careful not to romanticize his life: having
ended Part III with the dramatic climax of his Mediterranean voyage, he begins Part IV by saying, "In spite of the
foregoing pages, I have no romantic story to tell . . ." (p.
139). However, he does confess in the crucial Part V "that
for years I must have had something of an habitual notion,
though it was latent, and had never led me to distrust my
own convictions, that my mind had not found its ultimate
rest, and that in some sense or other I was on a journey" (pp.
214–215). He implies that this sense of odyssey became so

magnified on his Mediterranean voyage as to produce "Lead, Kindly Light" (*ibid.*). He speaks, in Part VI, of "the miles, over which my soul had to pass before it got to Rome . . ." (p. 264); and he does begin Part VII by comparing his conversion to "coming into port after a rough sea . . ." (p. 331).

Moreover, as he clearly indicates in Part II, Newman is conscious of two selves—"his past self and his present"— (p. 94), and Parts III–VI of the *Apologia* are offered as proof of the identity of "his past self"—proof to the reader as well as to the author, who "look[s] on mainly as a spectator . . ." (p. 12). Thus there is in the *Apologia* something of the pattern of certain Victorian novels, for example, *Great Expectations* and *The Way of All Flesh*. The narrator is, in fact, the protagonist, but at a distance and after an essential change has taken place. Newman, like the elder Pip (Dickens) and like Overton (Butler), views "his past self" "mainly as a spectator," aware that "his past self and his present" have distinguishable identities. The difference between them is the difference between doubt and "anxiety of heart," on the one hand, and "perfect peace and contentment," on the other; and the climactic act is, of course, recognition and acceptance.

One of the fascinating aspects of the *Apologia* as Newman unfolds it is the role of the "inward ear" in the progress from one spiritual stage to another. Thus in Part I, he speaks of "words [which] have been running in my head" (p. 77); in Part II, of "how a certain key . . . may cling to the mind" (p. 98); in Part III, "The words, 'Secretum meum mihi,' keep ringing in my ear . . ." (p. 105), and "Some portions of their teaching [Clement and Origen], magnificent in themselves, came like music to my inward ear . . ." (p. 128); in Part VI, " 'Obliviscere populum tuum et

domum patris tui,' has been in my ears for the last twelve
hours" (p. 327); and, of course, everyone remembers how
"the palmary words of St. Augustine"—"Securus judicat
orbis terrarum"—"kept ringing in [Newman's] ears" and
"absolutely pulverized" the theory of the *Via Media* (pp.
212–213).

Here we have, I believe, a significant key to the essential Newman, both as religionist and as stylist. He was
aurally oriented: He lived in a world of sound rather than
of sight. He heard himself speak, and his ear was the final
test of the quality of his writing. (In his essay on "Literature," he says that literature "addresses itself, in its primary
idea, to the ear, not to the eye.") Moreover, it was through
sound that his imagination was touched, and although he
was "determined to be guided, not by [his] imagination, but
by [his] reason" (p. 215), it was in fact his imagination
which guided him. The collapse of the *Via Media* provides
an example.

This particular issue has confused readers of the *Apologia,* and some have thought to catch Newman in a contra-
diction. For example, he says two things in two places in
this discussion: first, that the words of St. Augustine—
"Securus judicat orbis terrarum"—"absolutely pulverized"
the *Via Media* (pp. 212–213); two pages later he says that
"[d]own had come the *Via Media* as a definite theory or
scheme, under the blows of St. Leo" (p. 215). I think
Newman is very significantly *not* contradicting himself and
that here we have the key to much of his religious thought.
Since Augustine and Leo are involved in two different disputes—the Donatists held that the validity of the sacraments
depended on the spiritual condition of the minister, and
the Monophysites maintained the single nature of Christ—
it cannot have been the arguments for or against the various

positions that mattered. Rather, it must have been the question of the existence or non-existence of a universal authority that mattered. Thus Newman does not mean literally that he discovered he held the tenets of a Monophysite, but that, like the Monophysites, he was in rebellion against the possibility of a universal authority. The Donatists and the reformers of the sixteenth century were also thus. Therefore, he insists that if they were heretics, he too is a heretic. It was not Newman's reason which was first caught: it was his imagination. He had not been convinced by Leo's arguments *at first*. But Augustine's sentence—"Securus judicat orbis terrarum"—caught hold of his imagination. It bespoke the universal authority for which he yearned, and it kept ringing in his ear. Then, *after* his imagination had been captivated, Newman turned back to Leo, and Leo's *arguments* hammered away the V*ia Media* "as a definite theory or scheme." Newman found, as he says one must find, his first principles in faith; then he let argument supply the rational supports to faith.

Contemporary students need to be made aware of yet another aspect of the *Apologia*, namely the *quality* of the believing mind that it images forth. Quality, of course, is not absolute or absolutely perceptible, and therefore it cannot be clearly seen in isolation. Fortunately, we do not have to see it so, for there is another book with which it can be fairly compared. In 1850, Newman's brother, Francis William Newman, published his own autobiography, *Phases of Faith*. Its lack of present-day currency does not make it unfair game. When it first appeared, the *Spectator* called it "one of the most dangerous assaults upon theological Christianity, and indeed Biblical religion, that has ever been made"; and A. W. Benn, in his *History of English Rationalism*, pronounced its arguments "the most formidable direct attack

ever made against Christianity in England. . . ." [10] Even so,
perhaps Thackeray has given Francis William Newman more
immortality than he could guarantee for himself. Arthur
Pendennis says:

> I see [truth] in this man who worships by Act of Parlia-
> ment, and is rewarded with a silk apron and five thousand a
> year; in that man, who, driven fatally by the remorseless logic
> of his creed, gives up everything, friends, fame, dearest ties, clos-
> est vanities, the respect of an army of churchmen, the recog-
> nised position of a leader, and passes over, truth-impelled, to
> the enemy, in whose ranks he is ready to serve henceforth as a
> nameless private soldier:—I see the truth in that man, as I do
> in his brother, whose logic drives him to quite a different con-
> clusion, and who, after having passed a life in vain endeavours
> to reconcile an irreconcilable book, flings it at last down in
> despair, and declares, with tearful eyes, and hands up to Heaven,
> his revolt and recantation.[11]

These two brothers, born of the same parents but four
years apart and subject as children to the same environmental and educational influences, arrived at diametrically
opposed positions. John Henry became a Catholic priest;
Francis William disavowed Christianity itself.

If one asks himself how it happened this way to Francis
William Newman, the answer must be, I think, that he
yielded to the Liberalism that his brother was fighting;
that he accepted as critical and scientific a conclusion based
on principles that had not themselves been fully explored.
This is why, is it not, Macaulay can rightly be said to have
had no philosophy; why John Stuart Mill, whenever his
deeper sense of human nature forced him to depart from
his basic premises, got caught up in contradictions. It is this
which gives the reader of *Phases of Faith* a sense of chaos.

Francis William Newman is barbed and incisive and

hardheaded in his literalness, but his conclusions are as personal and accidental as Macaulay's. For example, at the time of his confirmation, he found everything in the service solemn except the Bishop, with his wig and artificial voice and manner; and from this *he realized* the impossibility of sympathizing "with those who imagined that Forms could command the Spirit." [12] (What he really means is that at that moment the idea occurred to him, and he immediately accepted it as incontrovertible fact.) He gave up the early Fathers who meant so much to his brother because, he says, "I could find no Articles, no Church Decrees, and no apostolic individual, whose rule over my understanding or conscience I could bear" (p. 16). After he had been to Persia as a lay missionary for two years, he returned to England and found himself the victim of social persecution because of his heterodoxy. This led him to two conclusions: that he would "love all good men from a distance, but never again . . . count on permanent friendship with any one, who was not himself cast out as a heretic"; and that *"spirituality is no adequate security for sound moral discernment"* (p. 42). This may be true, of course, but it is obvious that Newman has made no effort to locate the "idea" of spirituality or of morality. Further, Newman came to believe that there was no essential connection between theological views and religious living—"that if a man of partially unsound and visionary mind made the angel Gabriel a *fourth person* in the Godhead, it might cause no difference whatever in the actings of his spirit" (p. 54).

Newman had, of course, set himself the problem of adjusting the relative claims of human knowledge and divine revelation. Naturally, therefore, he turned to the question of religious evidences and logic. The apostles, he felt, had im-

bibed the outlook of their time: for example, John's men-
tality was that of Philo. Therefore, it is of fundamental importance to reassess the evidence that John accepted and to
analyze the reasoning with which he developed it. "Did he
see a sight, or hear a sound? or was it an inward impression?
and how does he distinguish it as divine?" (p. 90) Further,
to what extent could even a proved miracle be compelling
evidence against one's moral judgment? Suppose two men
—Nathaniel, a guileless saint, and Demas, a sharp world-
ling. If faith rests on miracles, the juggleries of a Simon
Magus will deceive the first, but not the second. It was to
the Nathaniels that Christianity in its origins was preached;
the only reliable ground for faith must be, not an accurate
judgment of the miraculous evidences, but the ordinary response of the individual's moral and spiritual sense (pp.
94–95). Of course, what Newman is doing here is assuming
that which, supposedly and in a show of fairness, he is dis-
interestedly investigating. He is setting aside faith, any conception that there is a moral rightness unknown to man's
reason, any willingness to admit of any validity in religion
not *given to it* by a cultivated understanding.

It would be possible to extend this list of exempla almost interminably, if there were any need. And my purpose
here is not to "debunk" Francis William Newman, although
that too would be valid, since he is representative of a whole
tradition of Biblical or religious rational criticism. This sort
of thing was very new in the Victorian period, and it was
taken very seriously, as indeed it should have been. But I
use it here to emphasize two things: first, that there is something distinctly qualitative in the differences between intellectual approaches to a problem; and, second, that John
Henry Newman's achievement, of keeping himself philo-

sophically intact among the delusions and spectacles of his age, is a very considerable factor in coming to a just appraisal of his achievement. It would not be so today: he would be left alone to pursue his sacramental values. It would not have been so fifty years before he lived: tradition was not yet seriously shifting. But for a supremely educated Englishman to come to a set of staunch philosophical principles among the shifting sands of theology between 1833 and 1845 was something positively phenomenal.

NOTES

1. (Spring, 1962), pp. 27–33.

2. *The Art of Newman's "Apologia"* (New Haven, 1945), p. 89. I trace much of my regard for Newman to a contemporary in graduate school, Dr. John Keating, of Kent State University.

3. *Letters and Correspondence of John Henry Newman during his Life in the English Church*, ed. Anne Mozley (London, 1891), I, 25.

4. Wilfrid Ward, *The Life of John Henry Cardinal Newman based on his Private Journals and Correspondence* (London, 1912), II, 400.

5. *Letters*, II, 250.

6. Ward, *Life*, I, 637.

7. As quoted from a transcript by the late Father Henry Tristram: *Newman: Prose and Poetry*, ed. Geoffrey Tillotson (Cambridge, Mass., 1957), p. 16.

8. *Lectures and Essays on University Subjects* (London, 1859), pp. 35ff.

9. All references to the *Apologia* are to Wilfrid Ward's edition (London, 1913). The quotation from Kingsley's pamphlet appears on page 25. Further references in this article appear in the text.

10. (London, 1906), II, 26. In the following comparison, especially, I owe a debt to Dr. Keating.

11. *The History of Pendennis* (London, 1884), II, 317.

12. (London, 1870), p. 2. All other references to this text are to this edition.

Sister Mary Baylon Lenz, O.S.F.:

THE RHETORIC OF NEWMAN'S
Apologia: *The Ethical Argument*

*L*ooking over the numerous studies of Newman and his
work, one is impressed with the predominance of theological and philosophical considerations and the comparatively
small emphasis given to studies of his literary achievement.
Fortunately the artistic aspects of his *Apologia pro Vita Sua*
have been explored by several critics within the past few
decades, but only Walter Houghton, in *The Art of Newman's Apologia,* has attempted an extended rhetorical study;
and this study was developed only in terms of specific techniques discussed in isolation from the continuity of the book.
Yet rhetorical structure is basic to the *Apologia,* and an
understanding of it opens further levels of meaning and ap-

preciation to the reader. Considering the importance of this rhetorical structure, we will here discuss one aspect: the way that Newman developed the ethical argument demonstrating his integrity as an Anglican while a member of that communion.

Recalling the events preceding the publication of the *Apologia*, one readily perceives the reasons for Newman's emphasis on rhetoric or persuasion, especially the ethical arguments, in his defense. In January, 1864, Charles Kingsley, writing in *Macmillan's Magazine*, openly attacked Newman's integrity: "Truth, for its own sake, had never been a virtue with the Roman clergy. Father Newman informs us that it need not, and on the whole ought not to be; that cunning is the weapon which heaven has given to the Saints wherewith to withstand the brute male force of the wicked world which marries and is given in marriage. Whether his notion be doctrinally correct or not, it is at least historically so." [1]

This charge demanded an answer from Newman, both for his own sake and that of the Catholic clergy whom Kingsley had also implicated in his accusation, but Newman realized that before he could gain an impartial hearing from his fellow Englishmen, he had to win their sympathetic understanding. Following his withdrawal from the active defense of the Anglican Church, and especially after his conversion to Rome in 1845, prejudicial views of his conduct had arisen; there was a vague popular impression that his conduct towards the Anglican Church while he was a member of it was inconsistent with Christian simplicity and uprightness.

Accurately appraising the situation, Newman adopted the necessary rhetorical means for persuading the English of his integrity. In the Aristotelian tradition, with which he was familiar, there are three modes of argument proper to the art of rhetoric: the logical, the ethical, and the pathetic. The logical emphasizes the reasonable quality of the proofs presented; the ethical concentrates on the character of the speaker; and the pathetic puts the audience into a receptive frame of mind.

Fully recognizing the illogical nature of prejudice, Newman realized that logical argument would be ineffectual. Since his integrity had been questioned, it was imperative that he first establish the goodness of his moral character; consequently, he emphasized the ethical argument. According to Aristotle, the ethical argument is effective "when the speech is so spoken as to make us think the speaker credible." [2] This credibility is achieved in three ways: through good sense, good moral character, and good will. In rhetoric, where the probable, not the certain, is the subject matter of discussion, good sense is especially important, for trust is more readily placed in the intelligent person, especially when that intelligence is allied with moral goodness. Consequently, the man who demonstrates wisdom through his arguments and judgments is more apt to be trusted. Good character is also a primary requisite for *ethos* and is manifested by the possession of and the practice of the virtues, such as humility, magnanimity, loyalty, fortitude, and earnestness. Finally, good will must be manifested towards the audience if the speaker is to gain its sympathetic attention. Newman employed all these methods for establishing the credibility of his defense, but this discussion will be limited to a few of the ways in which he persuaded the readers that he possessed a good moral character.

Since in 1864 the general feeling existed that Newman, during the final years of his Anglican career, had been "a 'Romanist' in Protestant livery and service," that he had been "doing the work of a hostile Church in the bosom of the English Establishment, and knew it, or ought to have known it" (*Apologia*, 95), he had first to convince his fellow Englishmen that during the time he was a member of the English Church, he had been faithful to this allegiance.

In Chapter I Newman initiates this image of loyalty by emphasizing his relationships with Anglicans. Covering the period of his youth from 1801 to 1833, this chapter begins the history of his mind by tracing the early development of his religious opinions. By showing that all of his early views, many of which persist in his Roman Catholic thinking, are the products of the teaching or the suggestion of men who are still admired and loved by the Anglicans, he proves that his early influences were English, not Roman. Newman carefully identifies with his proper position in the Church every person who was responsible for any contribution to his beliefs. "The human means of this beginning of divine faith in me" was "the Rev. Walter Mayers of Pembroke College, Oxford" (*Apologia*, 107). The author of the *Treatise on Apostolical Preaching*, through which Newman was led to give up his remaining Calvinism, was "Sumner, afterwards Archbishop of Canterbury," and Whately is recalled as "afterwards Archbishop of Dublin" (*Apologia*, 112, 111).

Furthermore, Newman points out that these were the men who brought him to the beliefs or practices for which he is now being criticized. It was Whately who taught Newman his methods of argument, which had since been considered to savor of the polemics of Rome. From Bishop Butler and Keble, he had gained the intellectual principles of sacramentalism and probability. In relation to Butler,

Newman comments: "Thus to Butler I trace those two principles of my teaching, which have led to a charge against me both of fancifulness and of scepticism" (*Apologia*, 114). With reference to Keble and probability, he writes: "On the second intellectual principle which I gained from Mr. Keble, I could say a great deal; if this were the place for it. It runs through very much that I have written, and has gained for me many hard names" (*Apologia*, 120–121). These are forceful appeals to the English sense of fair play; at the same time they illustrate the Anglican forces influencing his religious opinions.

Finally, Newman establishes an affinity between himself and his readers, the English public, through his appeal to a community of response and interest. Early in the chapter he supposes that "any reader of [Thomas] Scott's history and writings" would be struck by "his bold unworldliness and vigorous independence of mind." Having won his audience thus far, Newman continues: "He followed truth wherever it led him, beginning with Unitarianism, and ending in a zealous faith in the Holy Trinity. It was he who first planted deep in my mind that fundamental truth of religion" (*Apologia*, 109). Scott followed truth; he first impressed Newman with the truth of the Trinity. The implied conclusion: Newman likewise follows truth, not falsehood as Kingsley had suggested.

Similarly Newman identifies himself with the English public in his reference to Bishop Butler's *Analogy*, "the study of which has been to so many, as it was to me, an era in their religious opinions" (*Apologia*, 113). Nor was Newman unique in his problem of confronting inconsistent beliefs: "Hence came that conflict of mind, which so many have felt besides myself" (*Apologia*, 110).

Newman also appeals to his readers' pride, as Englishmen, in fellow Englishmen. In regard to Scott, he comments that his "resolute opposition to Antinomianism, and the minutely practical character of his writings . . . show him to be a true Englishman, and I deeply felt his influence" (*Apologia*, 109). Froude, to whom Newman owed so much that he could not enumerate the precise additions to his theological creed which he derived from him, "was an Englishman to the backbone in his severe adherence to the real and the concrete" (*Apologia*, 126).

To further establish the integrity of his character and his loyalty to the English Church during this period and to disprove the suspicions that he was hypocritically serving Rome, Newman disavows any early Catholic influence. As a child he was very superstitious and used to constantly cross himself on going into the dark. Where he derived this practice Newman cannot conjecture; certainly no one had ever spoken to him on the subject of the Catholic religion, which he only knew by name. Furthermore, his association of things Catholic with superstition supports his denials. As a climax to these disclaimers, Newman refers for verification of his statements to his brother Francis, a well-known freethinker: "My brother will bear witness how free the school was from Catholic ideas" (*Apologia*, 106).

The youth had not been indoctrinated with Catholic ideas: on the contrary, he had been carefully guarded from them. What of the maturing young man who was drawing the members of an incipient movement around himself? His attitude towards Catholics and Catholic services on his Mediterranean trip, in the critical year 1833, speaks for the entire period: "We kept clear of Catholics throughout our tour" (*Apologia*, 133). This conclusive statement is supported by a survey of every business contact with Catholics that he had during the trip; the matter-of-fact listing confirms the veracity of the writer and precludes a charge of self-delusion. In fact, Newman makes such a point of his separation from Catholics that it almost seems over-emphatic at times. To further intensify the impression of his total separation from everything Catholic, he concludes these references with an expression of his failure to understand the real Catholic spirit: "I saw nothing but what was external; of the hidden life of Catholics I knew nothing" (*Apologia*, 134). While further witnessing his alienation from Catholics, this allows for his later change of opinion, when he learned the inner spirit of Catholicism.

In Chapter I Newman traces the origin and development of his religious opinions, emphasizing the role of external influences, especially persons and books respected by the Anglicans, in their formation. In this way he establishes his allegiance to the Anglican position and his alienation from Roman Catholic influence. In Chapter II he recounts his association with the Oxford Movement and its role in his religious development. From the beginning of the Movement in 1833 until his final separation from it in 1841, Newman was loyally dedicated to its aim: defending the Anglican Church from Liberal attacks. He first establishes the Movement as a bulwark for the Church against the onslaught of Liberalism; then, by virtue of his association with it, his personal loyalty and unselfish dedication to the Anglican Church are simultaneously asserted. Through vivid diction, Newman sets up the opposition between Liberalism, the "specific danger which at that time was threatening the religion of the nation and its Church" and the Oxford Movement. Liberalism was the "calamity of the times"; it was an "assault . . . upon the old orthodoxy of Oxford and England"; it would "make shipwreck of Christian faith." The implications of these statements are climaxed in the Phaeton metaphor: "Since that time Phaeton has got into the chariot of the sun; we, alas! can only look on, and watch him down the steep of heaven. Meanwhile, the lands, which he is passing over, suffer from his driving" (*Apologia*, 139, 140, 158).

Because Newman was associated with the Movement dedicated to the protection of the established Church from these attacks, the reader is to conclude that he was a loyal member of the English Church during those years, and he reinforces this impression through the motif of his security in the Movement's position: "I had a supreme confidence in our cause; we were upholding that primitive Christianity which was delivered for all time by the early teachers of the Church, and which was registered and attested in the Anglican formularies and by the Anglican divines" (*Apologia*, 145). Moreover, his assurance was complemented by absolute rejection of the Roman cause: "Nor was it only that I had confidence in our cause, both in itself, and its polemical force, but also, on the other hand, I despised every rival system of doctrine and its arguments too" (*Apologia*, 146).

His conviction that his Anglican position was secure and that his opposition to Rome was unassailable made him certain nothing would destroy his belief. "And now I come to the very point, for which I have introduced the subject of my feelings about Rome. I felt such confidence in the substantial justice of the charges which I advanced against her, that I considered them to be a safeguard and an assurance that no harm could ever arise from the freest exposition of what I used to call Anglican principles" (*Apologia*, 156). Thus he counters the insinuations that he was working for Rome while a member of the Anglican communion.

Rather, he felt his Anglican position was so firm that it would withstand the forthright presentation of the Roman position and profit by it. He reasserts this security: "It was with this absolute persuasion on my mind that I fancied that there would be no rashness in giving to the world in fullest measure the teaching and the writings of the Fathers. I thought that the Church of England was substantially founded upon them" (*Apologia*, 156–157).

Not only was he attempting to defend the Church of England against her adversaries, but he wanted to strengthen her position through the formulation of a positive Anglican theology. "I wanted to bring out in a substantive form a living Church of England, in a position proper to herself, and founded on distinct principles; as far as paper could do it, as far as earnestly preaching it and influencing others towards it, could tend to make it a fact;—a living Church, made of flesh and blood, with voice, complexion, and motion and action, and a will of its own" (*Apologia*, 171).

Also contributing to the conception of Newman as a loyal Anglican are the references to his sense of duty towards the Church and his great reverence for, and obedience to, his Bishop. Duty urged him on to tasks that were distasteful to him. "As a matter, then, of simple conscience, though it went against my feelings, I felt it to be a duty to protest against the Church of Rome" (*Apologia*, 155). Opposition to Liberal tendencies was similarly an obligation, as were the writing of the *Prophetical Office*, in which he attempted to formulate a positive Anglican doctrine, and the writing of Tract 90, which was motivated by a desire to quiet the restlessness of those who liked neither the *Via Media* nor Newman's strong judgment against Rome.

This sense of duty was closely allied with his concept of obedience to his Bishop, which in turn was based on a reverence for the individual as a representative of God. "I loved to act as feeling myself in my Bishop's sight, as if it were the sight of God. It was one of my special supports and safeguards against myself; I could not go very wrong while I had reason to believe that I was in no respect displeasing him. It was not a mere formal obedience to rule that I put before me, but I desired to please him personally, as I considered him set over me by the Divine Hand. I was strict in observing my clerical engagements, not only because they *were* engagements, but because I considered myself simply as the servant and instrument of my Bishop" (*Apologia*, 152).

The proof that these sentiments were more than superficial was demonstrated in Newman's readiness to withdraw the Tracts if his Bishop judged this necessary: "And I offered to withdraw any of the Tracts over which I had control, if I were informed which were those to which your Lordship had objections. . . . Your Lordship did not think it necessary to proceed to such a measure, but I felt, and always have felt, that, if ever you determined on it, I was bound to obey" (*Apologia*, 176). This loyalty was severely challenged by the attack on Tract 90, yet Newman retained his respect and admiration for his Bishop in this trying situation: "I impute nothing whatever to him, he was ever most kind to me" (*Apologia*, 187).

Also contributing to the image of his loyalty to the Anglican Church is his denial of any self-seeking or desire for private gain through his association with the Movement, especially through leadership in it. He never wished to be anything "more than a leading author of a school" (*Apologia*, 159). When he wrote to his Bishop resigning his place in the Movement, his only regret was the anxiety caused for his Bishop; other than that he had nothing to be sorry for, because he had "never taken pleasure in seeming to be able to move a party" (*Apologia*, 188). He did have influence, but it was not sought after.

After having shown in Chapter I that the sources of his religious beliefs were gained from Anglicans, Newman continues to develop the image of his Anglican loyalty in Chapter II primarily through showing his connections with the Oxford Movement, which had been organized to defend the Anglican Church against Liberalism. Newman's confidence in the Movement and his efforts to formulate a positive Anglican position coupled with his absolute rejection of the Roman stand further develop the image. Likewise, his devotion to duty and to his Bishop contribute to this impression. Together all of these proofs of his fidelity to the Church of England help to counter the false prejudice which questioned his sincerity and integrity.

Chapter III covers some of the same years handled in Chapter II, but whereas in Chapter II Newman described his assurance in the Oxford Movement, now the focus is centered on the tensions that arose as his religious opinions were challenged, developed, and modified during these years, particularly as a result of the events of 1839 and 1841. He begins the chapter by reaffirming the conviction he had in 1839 of the superiority of the Anglican position and reasserting the supreme confidence which was a motif of Chapter II: "In the spring of 1839 my position in the Anglican Church was at its height. I had supreme confidence in my controversial *status*, and I had a great and still growing success, in recommending it to others" (*Apologia*, 192). But this certitude was shaken by questions arising during the study of the Monophysite history and for the first time he was faced with a doubt, "of the tenableness of Anglicanism"

(*Apologia*, 210). As the narrative progresses, the expression of doubt becomes correspondingly stronger. Finally, after the events of 1841, Newman states bluntly: "The Anglican Church might have the Apostolical succession, as had the Monophysites; but such acts as were in progress led me to the gravest suspicion, not that it would soon cease to be a Church, but that, since the 16th century, it had never been a Church all along" (*Apologia*, 238). Newman traces his gradually weakened stand from a peak of confidence to "the beginning of the end" (*Apologia*, 241).

In the context of this withdrawal from a positive defense of Anglicanism to a negative stand criticizing the social and political action of Rome, Newman's task of establishing his fidelity to the Anglican Church is even more difficult; but proportionate to the difficulty is the necessity that he demonstrate his loyalty. One method he employs is the frequent disavowal of any Roman allegiance or sympathy. At the opening of Chapter III he states: "Conscious as I was that my opinions in religion were not gained, as the world said, from Roman sources, but were, on the contrary, the birth of my own mind and of the circumstances in which I had been placed, I had a scorn of the imputations which were heaped upon me" (*Apologia*, 192). In fact, it seems that Newman's feelings during these years were prejudiced against Rome. For example, after showing that the issue of the Anglican-Roman controversy could be expressed as Apostolicity *versus* Catholicity, he comments: "However, in thus stating the matter, of course I do not wish it supposed that I allowed the note of Catholicity really to belong to Rome, to the disparagement of the Anglican Church." In concluding the explanation of his stand at that time he reasserts this view: "So much for our own claim to Catholicity, which is so perversely appropriated by our opponents to themselves" (*Apologia*, 204). As in many of the previous remarks, the tone conveys a confident attitude.

Newman's partiality for the English position was retained, though somewhat weakened, after 1839: "I was very averse to speaking against doctrines which might possibly turn out to be true, though at the time I had no reason for thinking they were." His last clause is a caution against the hasty conclusion that he was already on the Roman side. If further proof is needed, it can be found in his retention of his charges against Rome: "Yet I *did* still hold in substance all that I had said against the Church of Rome in my *Prophetical Office*" (*Apologia*, 219). It is even more obvious in his harsh indictment of the secular and political conduct of Rome: "I had a fulfillment before my eyes how the Court of Rome played fast and loose" (*Apologia*, 221).

Likewise significant in Newman's establishment of his loyalty to the Anglican Church is his description of his determination to find a position that he could reasonably defend; despite his growing uncertainty, he never considered leaving Anglicanism, but instead struggled to maintain his stand. After the force of Antiquity had been shattered for him, he sought a new basis for defending the English Church. "My first business then, was to examine the question carefully, and see, whether a great deal could not be said after all for the Anglican Church, in spite of its acknowledged shortcomings" (*Apologia*, 226). While recognizing deficiencies in the position, this passage expresses his loyalty and is especially convincing. Newman further develops this impression through the representation of his determination to be guided by reason. Yet despite this resolution he allowed prejudice to operate against Rome. For example, he admits that he could not throw off his antipathy towards the Vicar of Christ though already convinced in

1838 that the charge of the Pope's being anti-Christ "was almost one of the notes of the Church" (*Apologia*, 218). Furthermore, when he gives examples of his opposition to Rome's political conduct, he constantly speaks of it as a feeling: "This feeling led me into the excess of being very rude . . ." (*Apologia*, 221). "And here came in another feeling, of a personal nature . . ." (*Apologia*, 222). Thus, the reader is led to conclude that Newman had weighted all the odds against Rome and in favor of England—surely not the policy of a concealed Romanist.

But the most effective expression of Anglican fidelity is the explicit statement he makes when detailing his Littlemore plans. Having described his purchase of land and his intention of establishing a monastic house there, he concludes: "I mention it, because it shows how little I had really the idea at that time of ever leaving the Anglican Church" (*Apologia*, 228).

Closely allied to these arguments is his repeated insistence on his fidelity to duty. The impression is more emphatically conveyed in this chapter than in the previous one, for the difficulties opposing the fulfillment of duty are greater. Despite opposing forces, Newman adhered to his Anglican responsibilities as long as he could honestly do so. When the authors of the Tracts were being criticized for the extravagances of some disciples, Newman and others published *Plain Sermons* from a sense of duty so that "good should not be evil-spoken of" (*Apologia*, 198).

After his calm had been disturbed by the realization of the parallel between the heretical Monophysite position and the Anglican, a period of excitement followed, but later he was able to reflect more calmly, and then he had to "determine its logical value, and its bearing upon . . . duty" (*Apologia*, 213). In this new position, he realized that his main line of attack must be directed against "Rome's political and social line of action" (*Apologia*, 220) rather than her doctrine. Nevertheless, when forced by duty to do so at times, he felt obligated to speak out, though it distressed him. This duty was the command of his Bishop. "How can I help saying it, if I think it? and I *do* think it; my Bishop calls on me to say out what I think; and that is the long and short of it" (*Apologia*, 220).

Despite his uncertainty he was obligated to act in 1839. Three actions—the article on the Catholicity of the Anglican Church, Tract 90, and contemplation of the resignation of St. Mary's—represent his response to this sense of obligation. In fact, the writing of Tract 90 was a matter of life and death. He retained St. Mary's temporarily out of a sense of duty, which he explained to Keble: "Since you think I *may* go on, it seems to follow that, under the circumstances, I *ought* to do so" (*Apologia*, 231). And his last act as an Anglican, the writing of his letter of protest to the Bishop of Canterbury, sprang from a sense of duty. "I do this very serious act in obedience to my sense of duty. If the English Church is to enter on a new course, and assume a new aspect, it will be more pleasant to me hereafter to think, that I did not suffer so grievous an event to happen, without bearing witness against it" (*Apologia*, 239).

His fidelity to the Anglican Church is further revealed in his repeated references to well-known Anglican authorities. As Aristotle had stated, the calling up of witnesses, especially ancient ones who cannot be bribed, is an effective ethical argument. Early in the chapter Newman shows the relationship between his ideas and those of prominent Anglicans. Though admitting that he held a large bold system of religion, he claimed his right to do so by pointing out the previous Anglican divines who had also held these doctrines, naming each and his doctrine, and thus implying his own integrity. The passage reads like a litany of Anglican clergy and doctrines:

I claimed, in behalf of who would in the Anglican Church, the right of holding with Bramhall a comprecation with the Saints, and the Mass all but Transubstantiation with Andrewes, or with Hooker, that Transubstantiation itself is not a point for Churches to part Communion upon, or with Hammond that a General Council, truly such, never did, never shall err in a matter of faith, or with Bull that man had in paradise and lost on the fall, a supernatural habit of grace, or with Thorndike that penance is a propitiation for post-baptismal sin, or with Pearson that the all-powerful name of Jesus is no otherwise given than in the Catholic Church [*Apologia*, 192–193].

Explaining his idea of Catholicity as it would apply to the Anglican Church, Newman appeals to the authority of the *Epistles* of St. Ignatius to support his interpretation. In his explanation of Antiquity he refers to another authority, Vincentius of Lerins. When he narrates his ideas on investigating the Catholicity of the 39 Articles, he admits the crucial nature of the experiment even though the Catholic sense of the Articles had already been implied in the teaching of Andrewes or Beveridge. In his letter to Keble he admits that his preaching may move sympathies for Rome, but he allies himself with previous great preachers, Hooker, Taylor, Bull. As he had stated earlier, when he questioned the validity of some of his charges against Rome, he had aimed to ally himself with the Anglican divines, accepting their work implicitly. "I am troubled by doubts whether as it is, I have not, in what I have published, spoken too strongly against Rome, though I think I did it in a kind of faith, being determined to put myself into the English system, and say all that our divines said, whether I had fully weighed it or not." Then he comments in a colloquial way that implies much more than is actually stated: "I was sore about the great Anglican divines, as if they had taken me in, and made me say strong things, which facts did not justify" (*Apologia*, 219). These associations and appeals to authorities are brought to a climax in his identification with his English reading audience, quoted from a harsh attack on Rome: "We Englishmen like manliness, openness, consistency, truth" (*Apologia*, 223).

In this chapter Newman began the difficult task of convincing the English that he was honestly maintaining a position within the Anglican Church despite the challenges and doubts which arose during the years of 1839 to 1841. In developing the ethical image of his Anglican fidelity, therefore, Newman emphasizes four points: 1) disavowal of any Roman influence or inclination; 2) constant reassessment of his Anglican position in his effort to maintain a defensible stand; 3) fidelity to duty despite growing alienation from many fellow Anglicans; and 4) appeals to the parallels between his own thinking and many reputable Anglican authorities.

With Chapter IV and the narration of the crucial events of the years 1841 to 1845, when he completed his move from Canterbury to Rome, Newman faced a still greater challenge in answering the charge of concealed Romanism. To prove his loyalty to the Anglican Church as long as he was member of its communion, he continues many of the arguments developed in Chapter III. He repeatedly emphasizes his sense of duty. In the approximately thirty references to duty in the chapter, nearly every facet of his Anglican career is included. There were duties towards those whom he had brought into the Movement; there were duties to his Bishop and to the Anglican Church; duty in the light of his beliefs; duty in the fulfillment of his responsibilities in his profession; duty to himself. He continued his duties not only while active in the ministry but also after his resignation from active membership. These numerous examples of his sense of responsibility to the Church of England bear convincing testimony to his loyalty and forcefully repudiate the accusation of hypocritical duplicity.

Also as in Chapter III, evidence for his Anglican fidelity is found in his continued search for a position on which to base his belief in the Anglican teaching. Finding the basis of Antiquity and the *Via Media* destroyed by the arguments of Leo and Augustine, he turned to an investigation of the Note of Sanctity to show that England "had at least one of the necessary Notes, as fully as the Church of Rome" (*Apologia*, 248). When forced by the Bishops' attack on Tract 90 to abandon this position, he turned to his Samaria view. He felt an obligation to resign his living when he was unable to keep his trust to the Bishop, and he reasoned that his position in lay communion would be the best possible under the circumstances. But even then he continued to serve the Church of England in his efforts to keep men who were unsettled from going to Rome.

This effort to keep the youth from acting precipitately is one of the strongest arguments for his loyalty to the Church of England during this period. It is emphasized from the very opening statement of the chapter, when he outlines his position in 1841: "I kept back all persons who were disposed to go to Rome with all my might. And I kept them back for three or four reasons; 1. because what I could not in conscience do myself, I could not suffer them to do; 2. because I thought that in various cases they were acting under excitement; 3. because I had duties to my Bishop and to the Anglican Church; and 4. in some cases, because I had received from their Anglican parents or superiors direct charge of them" (*Apologia*, 246). He carefully outlines his position at various intervals and presents the true facts explaining the actions which puzzled the public and about which prejudicial rumor had arisen. One of the motives behind each of these actions—his residence at Littlemore, his withdrawal of the charges against Rome, and his resignation of St. Mary's—was his feeling of responsibility to the Church of England. The climax of this argument is in the narration of his resignation of St. Mary's; his final reason for resigning was the conversion to Catholicism of one of the young men at Littlemore. Despite the fact that Newman tried to hold the young man back, he considered this conversion a kind of betrayal of his Bishop and the Church of England. Newman summarized his reasoning: "I felt it impossible to remain any longer in the service of the Anglican Church when such a breach of trust, however little I had to do with it, would be laid at my door" (*Apologia*, 305).

This effort at holding young men back from Rome harmonizes with Newman's gradual withdrawal from influencing others in any other way than quieting them. When he worked with the Oxford Movement and was supremely confident in the position of the Anglican Church, he had been zealous in drawing others into her communion, but now, as his position was weakening, he realized that his first obligation was to gain certitude for himself. The circle of his influence narrowed from the wide activity of the period of the Oxford Movement until the conflict centered within his soul. He admits that he was drawn to Rome, were he to go by his feelings, but reason had to lead the way. In support of this position he quotes from a letter written in

1841: "That my *sympathies* have grown towards the religion of Rome I do not deny; that my *reasons* for *shunning* her communion have lessened or altered it would be difficult perhaps to prove. And I wish to go by reason, not by feeling" (*Apologia*, 282).

This sympathetic response to Rome was present in 1841, yet he did not join her communion until 1845; during these years, especially during the last two, his main problem was to gain certitude for himself through a reasoned approach. "I had one final advance of mind to accomplish, and one final step to take. That further advance of mind was to be able honestly to say that I was *certain* of the conclusions at which I had already arrived. That further step, imperative when such certitude was attained, was my *submission* to the Catholic Church. This submission did not take place till two full years after the resignation of my living in September 1843; nor could I have made it at an earlier day, without doubt and apprehension, that is, with any true conviction of mind or certitude" (*Apologia*, 306).

Where did his allegiance lie during this time? Was it then that the charges of concealed Romanism gained credence? This suspicion is answered with the simple but direct summary of the activities of these years: "In the interval, of which it remains to speak, viz. between the autumns of 1843 and 1845, I was in lay communion with the Church of England, attending its services as usual, and abstaining altogether from intercourse with Catholics, from their places of worship, and from those religious rites and usages, such as the Invocation of Saints, which are characteristics of their creed. I did all this on principle; for I never could understand how a man could be of two religions at once" (*Apologia*, 306).

Some of the so-called Roman additions still proved ob-

stacles to Newman at this time, and his forthright criticism
of them, his frank admission of his sympathy for the Catholic
position in other respects, and his loyal attendance of the
Anglican services illustrate his lingering English fidelity.
That his prolonged search for certitude was an effective
argument for this fidelity is evidenced by the words of Richard Hutton: "Nothing seems to me a greater proof of Newman's sincerity and fidelity to his own intellectual conviction than the long period of hesitation through which he
passed between 1841, when Tract 90 was condemned by
the almost unanimous acclamation of the Anglican Church,
and 1845 when he joined the Church of Rome." [3]

The arguments delineated thus far have been indirect
ways of answering the charge of concealed Romanism, but
Newman did not stop there. He issues several direct rebut-
tals. Quoting from a letter to Stanley Faber refuting this
very charge, Newman first of all clarifies his understanding
of the term. "By a 'concealed Romanist' I understand him
to mean one, who, professing to belong to the Church of
England, in his heart and will intends to benefit the Church
of Rome, at the expense of the Church of England" (*Apologia*, 279). Then, assuming the offensive, he summarizes
his changes of position during the ten years from 1835
to 1845. Though he gradually shifted from his stand during
the early years from a position where he "honestly wished
to benefit the Church of England at the expense of the
Church of Rome" to one immediately preceding his entry
into the Catholic Church (at which time he "was engaged
in writing a book (*Essay on Development*) in favour of the
Roman Church, and indirectly against the English"), at no
time did he intend "to benefit the Church of Rome, at
the expense of the Church of England" (*Apologia*, 279).
In other words, never during those ten years was he a hypo-

crite, professing one religion and supporting another, as had been charged.

One of the more obvious techniques employed by Newman to convey the truth of his personal integrity is his frequent quotation from letters written during the period. In Chapter IV sixty-one letters are used to support his statements; he repeatedly narrates the facts of the situation and then substantiates the statement of Newman the Catholic in 1864 with letters of Newman the Anglican of the 1840's. Besides giving an intimate picture of a soul searching for certitude, these letters are telling arguments for Newman's veracity. Letters written with no thought of publication are convincing witnesses to the truth of his statements, for one would have little reason for being dishonest when writing to intimate friends. Furthermore, the sincerity and intensity of the feelings, latent or expressed, vouch for the integrity of the writer. In the opening paragraph of the chapter Newman explicitly indicates his reason for using letters: "My narrative must be in great measure documentary, as I cannot rely on my memory, except for definite particulars, positive or negative" (*Apologia*, 245). In the preceding chapters, the documentation had been obtained primarily from his published works, but there was no published material to consult for these years. He quotes letters in which he was urging young men to consider more carefully before they go over to Rome, and letters to Catholic friends in which he continues to find fault with the Roman position, but possibly the most significant letters supporting his Anglican fidelity are two letters from the Bishop of Oxford and from Charles Marriott. In the midst of the suspicions circulating about Newman's activities at Littlemore, he received a letter from his Bishop expressing confidence in his integrity:

So many of the charges against yourself and your friends which I have seen in the public journals have been, within my own knowledge, false and calumnious, that I am not apt to pay much attention to what is asserted with respect to you in the newspapers. . . . I know you too well not to be aware that you are the last man living to attempt in my Diocese a revival of the Monastic orders (in anything approaching to the Romanist sense of the term) without previous communication with me,—or indeed that you should take upon yourself to originate any measure of importance without authority from the heads of the Church,—and therefore I at once exonerate you from the accusation brought against you by the newspaper [*Apologia*, 267–268].

Such a tribute to Newman's integrity, to his loyalty to the Anglican Church, and to his sense of responsibility, coming from his Superior is a powerful witness in his behalf.

A final, conclusive tribute to Newman's integrity is effectively placed immediately before the narrative of his conversion. A few months before his conversion, Charles Marriott wrote to Newman. His letter contains a testimonial to Newman's upright and unselfish dealings with the Anglican Church. Coming from an Anglican who was pained by Newman's actions, these words are especially convincing: "Your whole conduct towards the Church of England and towards us, who have striven and are still striving to seek after God for ourselves, and to revive true religion among others, under her authority and guidance, has been generous and considerate, and, were that word appropriate, dutiful, to a degree that I could scarcely have conceived possible, more unsparing of self than I could have thought nature could sustain" (*Apologia*, 324). In these words, the most direct ethical appeal Newman makes to his readers, he verges on pleading with them to believe him as others have done before.

Chapter IV concludes the history of Newman's Anglican years, and it brings together many of the techniques that he has used in the earlier chapters to depict his Anglican loyalty. He reaffirms his continued sense of duty even in the face of opposition and criticism from Anglican authority; he details his constant search for a position of security within the Anglican fold; he shows his loyalty to the Bishops despite their attacks. But in these final touches of his Anglican portrait, he adds the climactic touches: despite his own insecurity he held others back from going to Rome; he constantly considered the interests of the Church of England in his decisions; he demanded intellectual certitude before he accepted the position of Rome. In this chapter he directly refutes the charge of concealed Romanism by detailing his actions during the crucial years from 1835 to 1845, and shows his movement in its true character rather than the distorted image ordinarily presented to the public; he also answers this charge indirectly by clarifying the causes of his retraction and other actions which raised doubts in the minds of the English.

With Chapter IV Newman completes the history of his Anglican years and the delineation of his Anglican loyalty. In Chapter V, he briefly presents the peace of mind he has possessed since becoming a member of the Roman Catholic Church and gives direct, ordered treatment to Kingsley's specific charges. The first four chapters were necessary to win the sympathetic response of the English readers so that they would listen to the refutation that he presented in Chapter V.

Although this discussion has concentrated on those

aspects of his ethical arguments that developed the image of his loyalty to the Anglican Church, Newman presented other arguments, demonstrating his good moral character. He constantly emphasizes the verification of dates and facts, illustrating his love for truth, and his association with his friends, evidencing his magnanimity and loyalty towards them. Though the ethical argument dominates the work, logical and pathetic arguments support the ethical and fill out the picture of Newman as a man of sense and one considerate of others. But to discuss either the logical or the pathetic arguments in any detail would have to be the subject of another essay.

In his *Apologia* Newman has achieved classic excellence. Whether the work is primarily autobiographical or apologetic will continue to be debated, but the intrinsic merit of the work remains. In it Newman has fused autobiography and apology in a memorable way; he has convinced his readers of his integrity by presenting them with the true key to his life: an understanding of his actions and of his reasons for those actions.

NOTES

1. As quoted by John Henry Cardinal Newman, in *Apologia Pro Vita Sua. The Two Versions of 1864 and 1865*, ed. Wilfrid Ward (London, 1913), p. xx. All further references to the *Apologia* are cited in the text itself.

2. Aristotle, *Rhetoric*, trans. W. Rhys Roberts and Ingram Bywater (New York, 1954), 1356^a, 5.

3. Richard H. Hutton, *Cardinal Newman* (London, 1905), p. 152.

Francis X. Connolly: THE

Apologia: HISTORY, RHETORIC,

AND LITERATURE

In this paper I propose first to identify the place of the
Apologia in literary history at the present moment, second,
to explore some ambiguities that affect its reputation, and,
finally, to offer to historians of literature some grounds for
a more precise evaluation of the *Apologia* as literature. I
begin with the assumption that if the *Apologia* is not, in
F. L. Cross's words,[1] "probably the greatest autobiography
in the English language," it is a classic of some kind. I take
it for granted, too, that a literary classic is a classic for literary
reasons, and not because it presents accurate personal history, or accurate general history, or convincing arguments,
however important these elements are in the total evaluation

of the book. My third assumption is that the chief responsibilities of the literary historian are: (1) to place a classic in its precise historical context, and (2) more importantly, to describe just what kind of a classic it is.

Our first question is: What is the reputation of the *Apologia* today, a century after its publication?

Few critics or historians of literature contest the secure place of Newman's *Apologia* in the history of English literature. From the appearance of the first edition in 1864 to the most recent reprint of the edition of 1873, testimonies to the literary excellence of the *Apologia* have been virtually unanimous. The judgment in the *North British Review* for August, 1864, set a tone that has been echoed, with minor variations, to our own day. The writer begins with a melancholy complaint:

We can hardly regret the mistake or distortion which led him [Newman] to write the book which he has written. Both in matter and manner it recalls the *Confessions* of St. Augustine. In style it is a model of prose, racy, idiomatic English. The words have evidently flowed from his practised pen with an ease and rapidity only equalled by the grace of the forms into which they fall; and the composition, though bearing the marks of fiery haste, is a model of continuous and consecutive argument.[2]

Similar tributes to Newman's prose style gradually fixed the canon of praise. Whatever the religious or philosophical views of the writer (and many admired Newman's prose in inverse proportion to their assent to his convictions), most commentators called the *Apologia* a classic and Newman "an incomparable master of his art." [3] Praise of his "limpid suavity and grace" and mention of the autobiography as a "popular and widely influential" work that was "composed with infinite dignity and wit" appeared in encyclopaedic histories like Edmund Gosse's *English Literature: An Illustrated Record*.[4] In the *Dictionary of National Biography*, W. S. Lilly writes of the *Apologia* that "Few books have so triumphantly accomplished their purpose as that remarkable work."[5] Another representative opinion is expressed in the *Oxford Companion to English Literature:*

In the *Apologia* Newman has offered "an exposition written with the utmost simplicity and sincerity, and in a style of limpid clearness, of his spiritual history, and has obtained recognition as a literary masterpiece."[6]

But if the literary reputation of the *Apologia* is secure, it is also ambiguous. The chief reason for that ambiguity resides in the divided attention of the main commentators and critics. From the first reviews of the *Apologia* up to the present moment, writers have discussed the *what* and the *why* of the book, rather than the *how*; that is, its content and motivation rather than its structure and style. Newman's Victorian contemporaries praised Newman's simple, direct, graceful and musical style, but they rushed on to question the truth of his historical statements, the validity of his theological and philosophical arguments, and the interpretation of his mysterious personality. Similarly, many modern historians and critics continue to take the excellence of style for granted and to concentrate on "substantive" questions.

Thus, in *The Victorian Age in Literature*, G. K. Chesterton devotes approximately two pages to Newman's defense of faith and reason, and only the following suggestive sentence to his style.

"The quality of his [Newman's] literary style," he writes, "is so successful that it succeeds in escaping definition." [7] The one definitely literary allusion to the *Apologia* in Anton C. Pegis' introduction to the Modern Library Edition is this statement:

His story came forth from him with a royalty of language that is the permanent hallmark of Newman the man; for Newman had a genius as a writer to be faithful, in the elevation of his language, to the height of his theme. [8]

This comparative disregard for the literary aspects of the *Apologia* is understandable in a general history of literature or in a book intended for a wide reading public. Lack of literary emphasis is more significant, however, in an edition prepared for students of literature. In his introduction to the Riverside Edition of the *Apologia*, [9] A. Dwight Culler refers to literary qualities only in occasional descriptive epithets like "drama" and in an evaluative phrase like "brilliant passages." Like Chesterton and Pegis, Culler stresses the man, the milieu and the moment, rather than the book itself. This focus on Newman the man, on ideas and historical perspectives rather than on specifically literary qualities is the established procedure of most historians of literature. Even the better standard histories regard the *Apologia* not as a work of art but chiefly as a personal document or as an example of controversial rhetoric. [10]

True, some scholars have examined a few specifically literary traits of the *Apologia*. Lewis E. Gates, in the introduction to *Selections from the Prose Writings of John Henry Cardinal Newman*, 1895, is an outstanding exception to the general tendency of literary historians and anthologists. [11] In 1937 Fernande Tardivel examined the art of Newman's writings in a general study of his literary personality. [12] Walter E. Houghton first directed serious and prolonged attention to the study of form and style in the

Apologia in 1945.[13] In the same year, Charles F. Harrold devoted a chapter to the art of the *Apologia* in his *John Henry Newman: An Expository and Critical Study of His Mind, Thought and Art.*[14] Martin Svaglic pointed out the dramatic structure of the book in 1951.[15] Robert Colby suggested a poetic rather than a rhetorical approach to the *Apologia* in 1954.[16] Because of the literary emphasis of these and other studies we now understand more clearly that the *Apologia* is not only a work of rhetoric that aims at persuasion but also a notable achievement of the literary imagination. It is both argument *and* evocative reminiscence, dialectic *and* poetry, objective analysis *and* personal drama. But in choosing argument and dialectic as their presiding classification, most historians of literature have unintentionally slighted the literary reputation of the *Apologia.*

Let us say at once that the emphasis on the controversial aspects of the *Apologia* derives from the history of the text. The historian of literature faces an initial problem of considering various editions of the *Apologia.* The first edition (1864) comprises the seven pamphlets issued weekly from April 21 to June 2, 1864, and an appendix, published on June 16, containing Newman's "Answer in Detail to Mr. Kingsley's Accusations." Its full title, *Apologia Pro Vita Sua: Being a Reply to a Pamphlet entitled "What, then, does Dr. Newman mean?",* clearly stresses its controversial bearing.

In the second edition (1865) Newman deleted the first two parts dealing with Kingsley's charges, reduced the 119-page appendix to seven notes, altered the text slightly to remove ephemeral allusions, added a letter, and several supplemental notes, and composed an important preface. Most significantly Newman changed the title from *Apologia* etc., as stated above, to *History of My Religious Opinions* (see

p. v, 2nd ed.). The changes clearly suggested that since he had achieved his immediate controversial purpose, he now felt that the *Apologia* should be regarded chiefly as public and personal history.

In a third edition (1869),[17] Newman expanded the preface by providing extracts from Parts 1 and 2 of the first edition "in order to set before the reader the drift I had in writing my Volume." (P. xiv, 3rd ed.) In effect, while Newman restored to the third edition some of the details pertaining to the occasion of the *Apologia*, he offered those details less as arguments than as historical data on a controversy already half-dead.

In a fourth edition (1873) Newman made a few alterations, some additional notes, and changed the title to: *Apologia Pro Vita Sua: Being a History of His Religious Opinions.* This title, combining the principal phrase of the first edition and a slight modification (*His* for *My*) of the title of the second and third, suggests that, while Newman recognized the persistent apologetic strain, he placed the *Apologia* in the class of history and autobiography. The editions, or issues, of 1878, 1881, and 1886, all retain the title of the fourth edition.

This brief look at the various editions helps us to appreciate the problems of the historian of literature. If the historian concentrates on the edition of 1864 he is inclined to stress apology, that is, the dialectical skill with which Newman defended his own thought and conduct. If, on the other hand, he concentrates on the editions of 1865 or of 1886, the last published in Newman's lifetime, he is inclined to stress the autobiographical themes, that is, Newman's encounters with books, personalities, and movements, the succession of ironic reversals in his career, and the characterizations of the author, his friends, and associates. Hence, the historian of literature faces a crucial decision: whether to emphasize the element of controversy or the element of autobiography, or to treat each element with separate but equal attention. This decision involves more than the selection of the right edition. It requires the historian to decide what kind of book he takes the *Apologia* to be primarily, and what aspects are most important in a history of literature.

I suggest that the literary historian should regard the *Apologia* not only as objective history and controversial prose, but as an artistic autobiography and as the story of a soul. For, as Mr. Buckler suggests, in another essay in this volume, the *Apologia* ought to be presented "not only as the autobiography of an individual man, but also as a spiritual odyssey, even as a spiritual romance." [18]

That the *Apologia* is in part an objective history goes without saying. Among its other purposes, it aims to present a substantially accurate account of Newman's personal religious experiences and of the movements in which he took part. Newman was careful to confirm the accuracy of his story by consulting his own letters and those of his friends, by referring to contemporary notes, memorabilia, sermons and books; in short, by documenting his narrative whenever possible. Moreover, Newman's concern for historical accuracy continued even after he first published the *Apologia*. Thus, in 1865, he concluded his preface to the second edition with a reference to Frederick Oakeley's *Notes on the Tractarian Movement*. "This work," he wrote, "remarkably corroborates the substance of my narrative. . . ." [19] Like Newman, the historian should continue to re-examine and re-evaluate the *Apologia* as objective history by examining new evidence and by re-examining old evidence. He must continually search for a fresh consensus. Yet the historical elements of the *Apologia* do not explain why the book is, or should be, read as literature.

It is evident that the *Apologia* is a persuasive attempt to exculpate Newman and his fellow Catholic priests from the charge of lying. True, Newman himself wished he could erase the controversial elements from his book. But, as he wrote in 1865, "its original title of *Apologia* is too exactly borne out by its matter and structure . . . to allow of my indulging so natural a wish." [20] Hence, the *Apologia* may legitimately be studied for its rhetorical devices. Like Socrates, Newman attacked the general assumptions behind the formal charges, and employed the strategy of telling his own life story to better establish his own credibility and to exhibit the pathos of his situation. Like Socrates, too, he brought his dialectical skill to bear when he traced the reasoning that led him first to accept and then to reject the theology of the *Via Media*. Newman did not believe that one could convert or even explain by a syllogism, but he used rhetorical syllogisms with uncommon skill.

Newman availed himself of many other rhetorical devices, as Sister Mary Baylon Lenz points out in her paper *The Rhetoric of Newman's* Apologia.[21] Like Demosthenes in his *De Corona*, Newman presented his case dramatically, in a series of conflicts and solutions, and in the form of questions and answers, of soliloquies and imaginative visions or fictions. He interwove argument and history; he evoked from documents the authority of the speaking witness; he arranged the several chapters in a climactic order; he selected similes and metaphors with an exact sense of their power to illustrate the subject and to compel the emotions.

In short, Newman's arguments were presented less as

abstract reasons than as revelations of his state of mind
and soul. Note for instance the four concluding paragraphs
of Chapter I, entitled "History of My Religious Opinions to
the Year 1833." The drift of the "reasoning," itself a summary of Newman's career up to this date, is contained in the
sentences:

It was the success of the Liberal cause which fretted me in-
wardly. I became fierce against its instruments and its mani-
festations.[22]

How personally he resented the success of the Liberal
cause is powerfully supported by the instances he relates.
Newman could not bear to look at the French tricolor, to
him a symbol of revolutionary liberalism. When in Paris he
stayed indoors. He asked snappishly of Dr. Thomas Arnold,
when the liberal headmaster of Rugby was cited as an
authority for a view on the Christian interpretation of a
Scriptural text, "But is *he* a Christian?" Contrariwise, together with Hurrel Froude he chose as a motto for *Lyra
Apostolica* the saying of Achilles: "You shall know the difference now that I am back again." [23] Other verses from the
Aeneid and from Southey's *Thalaba the Destroyer* came to
his mind as expressions of his militant resistance to the
Liberal Movement. Even more to the point are Newman's
references to a mysterious sense of destiny. During his illness
in Sicily he suddenly burst out, "I shall not die." Later,
during a sudden fit of sobbing, he said to a servant, "I have
a work to do in England."

In these paragraphs are spontaneous confessions. By
recalling the personal fact, they *testify* to a conviction rather
than strive to *establish* a conviction.

If Newman was Demosthenian in his tendency to present ideas dramatically, he was Ciceronian in his cultivation

of a personal style. Like Cicero, he imparted to his sentences the rhythms, the pulsations of his own thought, making them "the faithful expression of his intense personality, attending on his inward world of thought as its very shadow." [24] Thus we experience in the *Apologia* sentences that express various shades of Newman's thought and feeling. His vigorous loyalty to Catholic principles is made evident by the affirmative rhythms in the following passage in which he contrasts the vigor of the primitive Church with the languor of the Church of England:

The self-conquest of her Ascetics, the patience of her Martyrs, the irresistible determination of her Bishops, the joyous swing of her advance, both exalted and abashed me. I said to myself, "Look on this picture and on that;" I felt affection for my own Church, but not tenderness; I felt dismay at her prospects, anger and scorn at her do-nothing perplexity. I thought that if Liberalism once got a footing within her, it was sure of the victory in the event. I saw that Reformation principles were powerless to rescue her. As to leaving her, the thought never crossed my imagination; still I ever kept before me that there was something greater than the Established Church, and that that was the Church Catholic and Apostolic, set up from the beginning, of which she was but the local presence and the organ. She was nothing, unless she was this. She must be dealt with strongly, or she would be lost. There was need of a second reformation.

Here the diction is sharply denotative, the syntax predominantly direct, the rhythm held in exact balance, the tone one of confidence in his mission. Other moods are reflected in other sentences. Thus, Newman begins Chapter III, in which he relates the catastrophe of the Tractarian Movement and the failure of his attempted *Via Media*, in slow and mournful periods, abundant with parenthetical

reservations. Note how the sentences below murmur sorrow-
fully at the memory of leaving home, of breaking strong and
tender ties. *Infandum dolorem,* Virgil's "unutterable woe,"
dominates the entire passage:

And now that I am about to trace, as far as I can, the course of
that great revolution of mind, which led me to leave my own
home, to which I was bound by so many strong and tender ties,
I feel overcome with the difficulty of satisfying myself in my
account of it, and have recoiled from the attempt, till the near
approach of the day, on which these lines must be given to the
world, forces me to set about the task. For who can know himself, and the multitude of subtle influences which act upon him?
And who can recollect, at the distance of twenty-five years, all
that he once knew about his thoughts and his deeds, and that,
during a portion of his life, when, even at the time, his observa-
tion, whether of himself or of the external world, was less than
before or after, by very reason of the perplexity and dismay which
weighed upon him,—when, in spite of the light given to him
according to his need amid his darkness, yet a darkness it emphatically was? And who can suddenly gird himself to a new
and anxious undertaking, which he might be able indeed to
perform well, were full and calm leisure allowed him to look
through every thing that he had written, whether in published
works or private letters? yet again, granting that calm contemplation of the past, in itself so desirable, who could afford to be
leisurely and deliberate, while he practises on himself a cruel
operation, the ripping up of old griefs, and the venturing again
upon the *infandum dolorem* of years, in which the stars of this
lower heaven were one by one going out?

The two passages we have just quoted are representative of many others in which Newman's style is the very
shadow of his intense, personal and developing thought.
Hence, while the *Apologia* will reward those who investigate
the rhetorical aspects of Newman's personal idiom, diction

and rhythm, it offers a greater reward to those who study Newman's style for clues to his personality. What Newman aimed chiefly to reveal was himself, not his skill in controversy. As he wrote in the ninth of his Oxford University Sermons, "When men understand what each other mean, they see, for the most part, that controversy is either superfluous or hopeless." [25]

That the *Apologia* was designed chiefly to make men understand what Newman meant is clearly evident from his own remarks. He described his meaning as one that was "simply personal and historical." He aimed to reveal "to high and low, young and old, what has gone on within me from my early years . . . my most private thoughts, I might even say the intercourse between myself and my Maker." [26] In short, the *Apologia* is an autobiography whose place in literature should be judged by its success or failure as personal revelation.

What are the criteria the literary historian should apply to an autobiography like the *Apologia?* With what other books should it be compared? One criterion is unity of theme. One book with which it should be compared is St. Augustine's *Confessions.* Just as St. Augustine proposed to exhibit in his own life the great mercy that led to his conversion, despite all his faults, so Newman shows how, committed to finding and doing God's will, he moved step by step from his conversion at fifteen, to an evangelical Christianity,[27] through his brief lapse into a kind of Liberalism,[28] towards acceptance of the Church of the Fathers,[29] thence to the attempted formulation of a Via Media in the Tractarian Movement,[30] finally, after a prolonged agony of introspection, to his "perfect peace and contentment" in the acceptance of the Catholic faith.[31]

Literary analysis of this development needs to regard not only the logical force of the incidental arguments, but also the effectiveness of Newman's representation of himself and his associates. It should look to the psychological accuracy of the writer's observations, to the vividness of his reconstruction of events, to his power to evoke the tone and nuance of intellectual and spiritual experience. Syntax, diction, and rhythm, the staples of rhetorical analysis, take on a new dimension when they are searched not for their persuasive intentions but for evidence of an organic relationship between style and the man.

Just before writing the *Apologia* Newman had explored this relationship in some detail both in his lectures on literature, contained in *The Idea of a University,* and in connection with his renewed interest in biography and autobiography. In 1857 he brought out a new edition of *The Church of the Fathers,* a volume consisting chiefly of biographical sketches of fourth-century saints, among them Sts. Basil, Gregory and Augustine. In 1859–1860 he wrote for the *Rambler* a short biography entitled "The Last Years of St. Chrysostom," planned as the first life in a book to be called *Ancient Saints.*[32] In a notable introduction to this biography, Newman set forth a theory of biography that, *mutatis mutandis,* may be invoked to explain the ideas that governed the composition of his own autobiography.

Newman confessed his delight in reading the lives of the saints, and his special affection for St. John Chrysostom:

He and the rest of them have written autobiography on a large scale; they have given us their histories, their thoughts, words, and actions in a number of goodly folios, productions which are in themselves some of their meritorious works.[33]

Newman placed great faith in the original words and actions recorded in letters, memoirs and spontaneous sayings. What he desired to know was not the mere facts but the motives, the inner life of his subjects.

> I repeat, what I want to trace and study is the real, hidden but human life, or the *interior*, as it is called of such glorious creations of God; and this I gain with difficulty from mere biographies. Those biographies are most valuable both as being true and being edifying; they are true to the letter, as far as they record facts and acts; I know it: but actions are not enough for sanctity; we must have saintly motives; and as to those motives, the actions themselves seldom carry the motives along with them. . . .
>
> On the other hand, when a saint is himself the speaker, he interprets his own action . . . his words are the index of his hidden life, as far as that life can be known to man, for "out of the abundance of the heart the mouth speaketh. . . ." [34]

Thus Newman studied language not only as the written record of facts and acts, but also as an index of motive and as unstudied self-manifestation. In controversial writing no less than in personal correspondence, he wrote that the ancient saints "mix up their own persons, natural and supernatural, with the didactic or polemical works which engaged them." [35]

Newman's views on biography and autobiography in the preceding passages are directly relevant to the *Apologia*. Newman clearly meant to manifest himself as well as to record facts and acts, to set forth his motives, his attitudes, his interpretation of events, his joys and his sorrows. Wayne Shumaker among others has pointed out that the last two paragraphs of Chapter IV are not bare narrative but interpretative autobiography. [36] In these representative passages, Newman conveys an awareness of past, present and future and suggests his deep personal sorrow by details carefully selected and artistically woven into the narrative.

I left Oxford for good on Monday, February 23, 1846. . . . Trinity had never been unkind to me. There used to be much snap-dragon growing on the walls opposite my freshman's rooms there, and I had for years taken it as the emblem of my own perpetual residence even unto death in my University. On the morning of the 23rd I left the Observatory. I have never seen Oxford since, excepting its spires, as they are seen from the railway.[37]

These sentences are notable for their brief but poignant self-revelation. Here indeed Newman's style, considered as selection of material, arrangement, diction, tone, and rhythm, is the measure of Newman himself.

What we have observed in the narrow range of a single passage may also be seen in the *Apologia* as a whole. The structure of the *Apologia*, it has been pointed out, is organized in a dramatic way, each chapter centering on "climactic moments, intensely felt and intensely remembered." [38] Newman presented himself in the role of the Christian soldier, "who, through defeat and submission, at last finds peace: a loving defeat ostensibly by his enemies but in reality by the 'sweet mysterious influence that called him on.' " [39] Thus Newman's climaxes may be seen as artistic epiphanies and his frequent muted military metaphors as benevolent ironies.

We have been saying that Newman's literary triumph is the achieved unity of his theme, the revelation of himself, the interior man, in the various stages of his voyage over rough seas into a haven of peace. Although this unity of theme deserves far more attention than we have attempted or suggested, we must hasten to mention another literary achievement with which it is closely related, namely his command of perspective.

Perspective, in this context, is the ability to represent "facts and acts" in their immediate circumstances and in their ultimate bearings. To maintain perspective is to be aware of the kind of truth that can only be discovered in the slow development of events through time, the kind of truth that, once vividly grasped, "rides time like riding a river." [40] Newman knew himself and expressed himself both as a creature in time and as a soul isolated from time. Thus while his *Apologia* is in one sense a record of growth and change, in another sense it testifies to a permanent personal identity. Early in the *Apologia*, Newman noted the importance of his conversion at the age of sixteen. This inward conversion, he wrote, made him "rest in the thought of two and two only absolute and luminously self-evident beings, myself and my Creator. . . ." [41] This consciousness remained with him throughout his life. Hence, while he could speak of a particular event in his life or the course of events during various periods of his life as unutterably sorrowful, at the same time he could say, as he said of the affair of the Jerusalem archbishopric, "I [think it] one of the greatest of mercies. It brought me on to the beginning of the end." [42]

Command of perspective results not only in a spiritual detachment that can simultaneously present actual events *sub specie temporis* and *sub specie aeternitatis*. It also encourages the artistic use of paradox. Thus Newman can write a suspenseful account of his spiritual agonies, as he does in Chapter IV where the imagery of the death-bed sets the tone, and yet, by command of perspective, evoke joy as well as sorrow.

Just how Newman achieves this paradoxical effect it is

the business of the literary historian to explore. He may well find that Newman's method of narration may be compared to that of the epic poem. For the *Apologia* recounts the perils of a spiritual Ulysses pursuing a kindly light to an ultimate haven. Its predominant emotion is that of an infinite pathos, the *infandum dolorem* of Virgil, that rises like a sigh from the contemplation of broken hopes, lost friendships and the pain of failure. Not unlike Hamlet, Newman broods over a world out of joint, in which he, "upon the imperious call of duty," [43] must play a part.

But if that world "is out of joint," as he wrote, "with the purposes of its Creator," and thus an occasion for grief, the Divine Will is still present, as ready to do for all what It has done for him. The tone of pathos is accompanied by the more energetic tone of hope. Hence at the conclusion of the *Apologia*, after a filial tribute to St. Philip, and a name by name recognition of his Oratorian brothers, Newman recalls his former Oxford friends and counsellors. Of them, and those whom they represent, he wrote:

And I earnestly pray for this whole company, with a hope against hope, that all of us, who once were so united, and so happy in our union, may even now be brought at length, by the Power of the Divine Will, into One Fold and under One Shepherd.[44]

If the *Apologia* is a permanent classic, it has achieved that status because it is the artistic representation of the growth of a soul instinct with the universal emotions of hope and fear, sadness and joy; because it communicates to those who read it the shape and the meaning of man. These are the values that, I believe, the historian of literature ought to point out with decisive emphasis.

NOTES

1. F. L. Cross, *John Henry Newman* (London, 1933), p. 132. It should be noted in passing that Cross's praise of Newman's art does not extend to the truthfulness of the *Apologia* as a whole. According to Cross, Newman's representation of truth is in error "in the way the whole drama is staged." P. 133.

2. *North British Review*, Vol. 41 (August 1864), 87. The tribute continues: "The subject is . . . the history of a singularly pure and noble and tender soul, struggling towards the light, in obedience to the laws of its own nature, through perplexity and darkness, through doubt and difficulty, through fightings without and fears within. . . . It recalls most vividly 'the image of that slight, spare form, so well known . . . that countenance so severe, and yet so tender; the sound of that thin but sweet voice, that peculiar intonation, that simple but studied delivery, which seemed to carry the words of the preacher straight to the hearts of the eager listeners who thronged the benches of St. Mary's.' "

3. W. H. Hutton, *Cambridge History of English Literature* (1916), XII, 280–308.

4. (New York, 1923.) The quotations are from Vol. IV, pp. 265, 267.

5. Vol. 14, p. 346.

6. Ed. Sir Paul Henry (1946), p. 554.

7. (Notre Dame, 1962), p. 22.

8. (New York, 1950), pp. xiii, xiv.

9. (Boston, 1956), pp. vii–xix.

10. Cf. S. C. Chew in *A Literary History of England*, ed. A. C. Baugh (New York, 1948), pp. 1294–1295, and *The Norton Anthology of English Literature*, ed. G. H. Ford (New York, 1962), pp. 1072–1074.

11. See particularly his remarks on p. xxii ff, where he refers to the specifically literary qualities of the *Apologia*.

12. *La Personnalité Littéraire de Newman* (Paris, 1937).

13. *The Art of Newman's "Apologia"* (New Haven, 1945).

14. See particularly Chapter XII, pp. 308–312.

15. See Martin J. Svaglic, "The Structure of Newman's *Apologia*," *Victorian Literature*, ed. A. Wright (New York, 1961), pp. 225–237. Although Svaglic regards the *Apologia* "primarily a work of rhetoric designed to persuade a body of readers . . . that Newman . . . was a man not of dishonesty but integrity" (p. 225), he dwells chiefly upon the elements of dramatic structure and style.

16. "The Poetical Structure of Newman's *Apologia*," *Journal of Religion*, Vol. 33 (January 1953), 47–57.

17. I have called the issue of 1869 a third edition because of the important shift in emphasis explained in this paper. The problem of distinguishing between editions and impressions or issues is explained in M. J. Svaglic's "The Revision of Newman's *Apologia*," *Modern Philology*, L (August 1952), 43–49. See particularly notes 4 and 5 on p. 44.

18. P. 70.

19. *Apologia*, p. 488. (All references to the *Apologia* are to the Oxford edition of Wilfrid Ward, 1913.)

20. *Ibid.*, p. 483.

21. Pp. 80–104.

22. *Apologia*, p. 134. The next quotation is on the same page.

23. *Ibid.*, p. 135. The next two quotations are on the same page.

24. "Literature" in *The Idea of a University*, p. 276.

25. P. 193.

26. *Apologia*, p. 101.

27. *Ibid.*, p. 107ff.

28. *Ibid.,* p. 116ff.

29. *Ibid.,* p. 127ff.

30. *Ibid.,* p. 140ff.

31. *Ibid.,* p. 331.

32. *Ancient Saints* was never completed. "The Last Years of St. Chrysostom" appears in *Historical Sketches,* Vol. II.

33. *Historical Sketches,* II, 218.

34. *Ibid.,* p. 219.

35. *Ibid.,* pp. 220–221.

36. "English Autobiography: Its Emergence, Material and Form," *Univ. of California Publications in English* (Berkeley, 1954), pp. 112–113.

37. *Apologia,* p. 327.

38. Houghton, p. 61.

39. Svaglic in *Victorian Literature,* ed. A. Wright, p. 231. The quoted phrase is from Newman's *Sermons Preached on Various Occasions,* p. 178.

40. G. M. Hopkins, *Poems of Gerard Manley Hopkins* (New York, 1948), p. 55, stanza 6.

41. *Apologia,* p. 108.

42. *Ibid.,* p. 241.

43. *Ibid.,* p. 192.

44. *Ibid.,* p. 372.

Hugo M. de Achaval, S.J.: THEO-
LOGICAL IMPLICATIONS
IN THE *Apologia*

A hundred years ago, in very dramatic circumstances, a
man was compelled to open his soul before a whole nation,
unless he preferred to be thought a liar and to confirm by
his silence the charges made against him, for more than
twenty years, by those who, after being his accusers, were
turned into the judges of his case. The man was Newman;
the judges, the whole of England. The man was acquitted.

In a few lines we have the moral of the *Apologia*. The
following few pages will be enough to bring out its theological implications. Since it is an Apologia, a history of Newman's religious opinions, it is not surprising that a theology
is to be found in it, since every religion requires some theo-

logical basis, and, on the other hand, every religious individual is in some sense a theologian. Its moral and its argument give us the starting point from which our inquiry is to be made. The everlasting conflict between reason and faith, nature and grace, freedom and law, self and world, man and God, finds in Newman's *Apologia* one of the clearest and most crystalline expressions ever attained. Few people can plumb their souls as he did. Newman's lifelong effort to realize the visible and the unseen world, his experience of the human and divine, his leading position in the struggle between Christianity and rationalism, made the issue prophetical and actual. He exhibits not a theory but a life, not a "notional" but a "real" argument founded on the voice of conscience, urgently calling him to make a tremendous change of mind. It calls him to lose and at the same time to gain whatever a man can lose and gain in this life on the basis of a conviction that religious truth cannot be gained outside the Catholic religion and that when a man is so enlightened, not to act accordingly would be a sin against light.

Although Newman was a Christian from the beginning, he only became fully aware of the fact at the age of fifteen. "I was brought up," he writes in the first page of his *Apologia*, "from a child to take great delight in reading the Bible; but I had no formed religious convictions till I was fifteen. Of course I had a perfect knowledge of my Catechism." When he was made Cardinal he recalled that in his youth Christianity was the law of the land.

When a man realizes what it is to be a man and finds himself being one, he begins to be other than what he was before. So with Newman's conversion of 1816. He realized what it was to be a man, what it meant to be a Christian, and at the same time he became both, and in such a way that he could "look back at the end of seventy years as if on another person." [1] His conversion was a return to, a renewing of principles under the power of the Holy Spirit, which he had already felt, and in a certain measure acted upon before his conversion. It was a returning to that religion of the Bible whose description is given in the *Grammar of Assent*.[2] There was one difference: Instead of a notional assent he now gave a real assent to Biblical truths. He rested in, as he tells us in the *Apologia*, "The thought of two and only two absolute and luminously self-evident beings, myself and my Creator" [3] or, as he phrased it in his journal:

The reality of conversion: as cutting at the root of doubt, providing a chain between God and the soul (i.e., with every link complete) I know I am right. How do you know it? I know I know. How? I know I know I know etc. etc.[4]

The *Grammar of Assent* is intended to show the full meaning of this "I know I know." The author openly confesses:

Were it not for this voice, speaking so clearly in my conscience and my heart, I should be an atheist, or a pantheist, or a polytheist when I looked into the world. I am speaking for myself only; and I am far from denying the real force of the arguments in proof of a God, drawn from the general facts of the human society and the course of history.[5]

Conscience comes first, teaching us natural religion, which consists in "the knowledge of God, of His Will, and of our duties towards Him." Natural religion is a preparation for revealed religion, at least by "the anticipation which it creates, that a Revelation will be given. That earnest desire of it, which religious minds cherish, leads the way to the expectation of it." So Newman some years later expressed it in the *Grammar of Assent*.[6] In the *Apologia* he had already outlined the existential connection between natural and revealed religion:

And thus I was led on to examine more attentively what I doubt not was in my thoughts long before, viz., the concatenation of argument by which the mind ascends from its first to its final religious idea; and I came to the conclusion that there is no medium, in true philosophy, between Atheism and Catholicity, and that a perfectly consistent mind, under those circumstances in which it finds itself here below, must embrace either the one or the other. And I hold this still: I am a Catholic by virtue of my believing in a God; and if I am asked why I believe in a God, I answer that it is because I believe in myself, for I feel it impossible to believe in my own existence (and of that fact I am quite sure) without believing in the existence of Him, who lives as a Personal, All-seeing, All-judging Being in my conscience.[7]

As I am not writing an apologia of the *Apologia*, I may be excused from discussing here the value of Newman's argument. I assume that his teaching can withstand a rigorous examination. But it must be judged on its own terms, and not according to preconceived standards of scholasticism. Newman's starting point is conscience, not reason. Only once—as far as I know—did Newman try to present a logical proof for God's existence. That was shortly after his return from Rome, in a sermon on "the Mystery of Divine Condescension."[8]

Nobody, perhaps, has written stronger words against reason than Newman, and at the same time, as the author of *The Idea of a University*, he praised reason. One apparent anomaly vanishes if we keep in mind the distinction he maintained between right reason and fallen reason, a distinction canonized by the First Vatican Council. In the *Apologia* he enunciated it as follows:

I have no intention at all of denying, that truth is the real object of our reason, and that, if it does not attain to truth, either the premiss or the process is in fault; but I am not speaking here of right reason, but of reason as it acts in fact and concretely in fallen man. I know that even the unaided reason, when correctly exercised, leads to a belief in God, in the immortality of the soul, and in a future retribution; but I am considering the faculty of reason actually and historically; and in this point of view, I do not think I am wrong in saying that its tendency is towards a simple unbelief in matters of religion. . . .[9]

With conscience however it is different:

Conscience is nearer to me than any other means of knowledge . . . and being carried about by every individual in his own breast, and requiring nothing besides itself, it is thus adapted for the communication to each separately of that knowledge which is most momentaneous to him individually,—adapted for the use of all classes and conditions of men, for high and low, young and old, men and women, independently of books, of educated reasoning, of physical knowledge, or of philosophy. Conscience, too, teaches us, not only that God is, but what He is; it provides for the mind a real image of Him, as a medium of worship; it gives us a rule of right and wrong, as being His rule, and a code of moral duties. Moreover, it is so constituted that, if obeyed, it becomes clearer in its injunctions, and wider in their range, and corrects and completes the accidental feebleness of its initial teachings. Conscience, then, considered as our guide, is fully furnished for its office.[10]

For this and similar statements, Newman was accused of "metaphysical or philosophical scepticism." Replying to Principal Fairbairn (*Stray Essays*, 1890) he maintained that not only for Catholics but for everybody, reason cannot master the whole of reality. Mystery is the boundary of reason.

After all, the Theist needs faith as well as the Christian. All religion has its mysteries, and all mysteries are correlative with faith; when faith is absent, the action of relentless "reason," under the assumption of educated society, passes (as I have given offence by asserting) from Catholicity to Theism, and from Theism to a "materialistic cause of all things." [11]

Without faith it is impossible to please God. But faith is impossible without conscience. Faith is not a question; it is an answer, for which we are responsible; and responsibility is a question of conscience, not of reason.

Newman's conversion was his answer—through a real assent—to the Divine Revelation contained in the Bible. Revelation is not a matter of words but of things and facts. The first fact is that of God's existence. The God of conscience is the same as the God of the Bible, the God of Abraham, Isaac and Jacob, the Father of Our Lord Jesus Christ. There are arguments to prove it, as there are arguments to prove one's existence, but Newman needed not argument to be sure of it:

I have changed in many things: in this I have not. From the age of fifteen, dogma has been the fundamental principle of my religion: I know no other religion; I cannot enter into the idea of any other sort of religion; religion, as a mere sentiment, is to me a dream and a mockery. As well can there be filial love without the fact of a father, as devotion without the fact of a Supreme Being. What I held in 1816, I held in 1833, and I hold in 1864. [12]

Natural Religion leads to Faith. Faith is its perfection. The God of Conscience is consequently the God of Grace as well.

A question arises: What about man? If conscience testifies to all men that they are sinners, that God is primarily a judge, a lawgiver, and if faith confirms the testimony of conscience, can Newman be said to be a humanist, and, if so, what kind of humanist is he? The author of *The Idea of a University* has been called a humanist, but is the author of the *Apologia*, the Parochial Sermons, and the University Sermons a humanist? Certainly his harsh sayings against reason and the world are not the sayings of a humanist, in the ambiguous and common sense given to the word, that is, one who speaks of the grandeur of the human race and human deeds. Certainly Newman is not to be compared with Jean Jacques Rousseau; nor is he a humanist of the kind of Jean-Paul Sartre. But he is a humanist in the only sense that a Christian can be said to be one, that is, a man who maintains the dogma of original sin and its tremendous consequences and at the same time affirms the freedom of man to acknowledge and receive the gift conveyed by the Incarnation of the Son of God Himself. His is the humanism of a man who feels deeply the abnormal condition of man and tries to do his best to help it. Thus Newman writes in the *Apologia*:

If I looked into a mirror, and did not see my face, I should have the sort of feeling which actually comes upon me, when I look into this living busy world, and see no reflection of its Creator. . . . What shall be said to this heart-piercing, reason-bewildering fact? I can only answer, that either there is no Creator, or this living society of men is in a true sense discarded from His presence. . . . And so I argue about the world; *if* there be a God, *since* there is a God, the human race is implicated in some terrible aboriginal calamity. It is out of joint with the purposes of its Creator. This is a fact, a fact as true as the fact of its existence; and thus the doctrine of what is theologically called original sin becomes to me almost as certain as that the world exists, and as the existence of God.[13]

Again, Newman's argument may be discussed by those theologians who hold that original sin cannot be known without revelation. It is not certain that St. Augustine and St. Thomas would be against Newman. Nor is his position irreconcilable with the doctrinal opinion that says man could be created in the same condition in which he is found today. In the latter case, the absence of grace would not be degradation or a loss as it is, but only a gift not given at all. Perhaps other gifts might be given in its place. Newman himself was aware that the doctrine of original sin is harder to believe than the doctrine of the Immaculate Conception:

Many, many other doctrines are far harder than the Immaculate Conception. The doctrine of Original Sin is indefinitely harder. Mary just has *not* this difficulty. It is *no* difficulty to believe that a soul is united to the flesh *without* original sin; the great mystery is that any, that millions on millions, are born with it. Our teaching about Mary has just one difficulty less than our teaching about the state of mankind generally.[14]

A humanist is not one who only speaks beautifully of man, but one who speaks the truth about man. Is he a true humanist who puts man above God, destroying man, or he who puts God in the first place and acknowledges man's capacity to attain God, through Jesus Christ? St. Paul was a humanist writing to the Philippians and writing to the Romans too. Newman in the *Apologia* reveals a Pauline spirit.

If Newman had written only the *Apologia*, readers might be puzzled by a seemingly odd fact: the *Apologia* does not speak of Christ. In his *Index to the Works of Newman*, Fr. Rickaby found no place in the *Apologia* worth noting under the name of Christ. However, the *Apologia*, like the *Confessions of St. Augustine,* is full of Christ. The conversion of 1816 made Newman a Christian; that of 1845, a Catholic. Newman's whole life was a Christian life. Many people hope to see Newman officially declared a saint, that is, Christ's Confessor. How can one reconcile the apparent anomaly?

If a Christian is a man who believes and follows Christ's doctrine; obeys Christ's Commandments; if he is a man for whom to live is Christ, according to St. Paul, is it true that Newman does not speak of Christ in the *Apologia?* Christianity after all is not a question of words but of facts; not a subscription to a series of articles or propositions, but a response to a large philosophy, a view, a reality, the assumption of a fact, the entrance of the whole man into a new order of existence. Granted there is a *Depositum Fidei,* but what is meant by that term? Newman asked that question and answered it: "Is it a list of articles that can be numbered? no, it is a large philosophy; all parts of which are connected together, and in a certain sense correlative together, so that he who really knows one part, may be said to know all, as *ex pede Herculem*." [15] Like most of Newman's writings, the *Apologia* is an occasional work. But in it there is hardly a line not in a certain sense connected and correlated with the central idea, the leading idea of Newman's life: Christ. I think this will become more evident to the reader of the *Apologia* if he examines carefully what Newman set down as the leading idea of Christianity, when he prepared the later edition of the *Development of Christian Doctrine.* The leading idea is, he says, the Incarnation, as declared by the inspired writers, especially St. John, first in brief, as an evangelist's absolute enunciation, "The Word was made flesh and dwelt among us, full of grace and truth," and then, in a more didactic tone,

as a Pastor of Our Lord's flock, "That which was from
the beginning, which we have heard, which we have seen
with our eyes, which we have looked upon, and our hands
have handled, of the Word of life, that declare we to
you." From announcements such as these, there follows,
according to Newman, "The principle of *dogma*, that is,
supernatural truths irrevocably committed to human language, imperfect because it is human, but definitive and
necessary because given from above," [16] or, to quote the
words he used in the first rough sketch made of the principle
in 1877, "Dogma, from the very form of St. John's words, is a
second principle of Christianity, that is, supernatural truth
definitively committed to human language, with an expression imperfect, indeed, because human language, but definitive and imperative, because it is given us from heaven." [17]
Words are the expression of an idea; the idea stands for a
thing or a fact. Dogma is the expression made by the Church
and proposed to our faith, of a thing or a fact, of which the
idea is expressed in logical terms by words. But as St.
Thomas said, *"actus credentis non terminatur ad ennun-
tiabile sed ad rem."* [18] Newman's formula is shorter: "Revelation is not of words."

The second principle Newman draws from the Incarnation as the leading idea of Christianity is "the principle of
faith, which is the correlative of dogma, being the absolute
acceptance of the divine Word with an internal assent, in
opposition to the informations, if such, of sight and reason."
Or, as it is said in the aforementioned first sketch of these
principles, "the most primary characteristic of Christianity is
faith, as contrasted with sight and sense, for we could not
learn of an Incarnation, except by means of Divine Revelation, and of Revelation the correlative is Faith."

The third principle that Newman deduced from the

Incarnation is that of theology: "Faith, being an act of the intellect, opens a way for inquiry, comparison and inference, that is, for science in religion, in subservience to itself; this is the principle of *theology*." As we are considering Newman's intellect at work, let us add here the first reaction of the principle: "Faith implies the exercise of (reason, erased; mind, erased) intellect, for brute animals cannot have faith; a dogma too, being a logical proposition, opens a way to science in religion, suggests (implies) to us that in subordination to faith, reason has in Christianity, not only its exercise, but its use. Thus St. Luke tells us: 'Mary kept all these things, pondering them in her heart.' "

With St. Augustine Newman holds theology to be "*de divinis philosophare*." But no confusion is made between theology and religion: the science of religion is not religion. Knowledge is good, but life is better. Knowledge for life; life for action; action for God, is Newman's hierarchy of values.

The fourth principle declares: "The doctrine of the Incarnation is the announcement of a divine gift conveyed in a material and visible medium, it being thus that heaven and earth are in the Incarnation united. That is, it establishes in the very idea of Christianity the *sacramental* principle as its characteristic." The first, less elaborated statement of the principle reads: "The doctrine of the Incarnation is of a sacramental nature, that is, a divine gift conveyed through an earthly and visible channel (means), it being by this use of Sacraments that heaven and earth are in the Incarnation united. He who first made a material body of His own, proceeded to use matter as His means of blessing, as the sentence continues (according to the word) 'The word was made flesh and dwelt among us, full of grace and truth.' "

In the *Apologia's* first chapter we are told of the genesis of these principles and their development. This one, accepted from childhood, was impressed more deeply upon his consciousness through reading the Alexandrian Fathers and Butler's *Analogy*. Newman felt intensely the need to get the full reality behind the signs of the visible world, to contemplate and find God's presence in all things.

Fifthly, Newman says: "Another principle involved in the doctrine of the Incarnation, viewed as taught or as dogmatic, is the necessary use of language, e.g., of the text of Scripture, in a second or *mystical sense*. Words must be made to express new ideas, and are invested with a sacramental office." Newman's original reads: "The sacramental principle necessarily belongs to (is necessarily extended to) the written word, that is (to revelation as written, erased) to the language (medium) under which the revelation is conveyed. This principle of the mystical sense—of which I have accidentally spoken above—is consecrated by Our Lord as His rule of teaching. His announcement, to take one instance out from many, of His resurrection, because taken literally by His enemies, is called by the Evangelist, false witness: 'Destroy this Temple. . . .' "

The mystical sense, the *sensus plenior*, the spiritual sense, the sense of Holy Scripture, its Inspiration, or the problem as stated in Newman's own words is not only a modern problem but an everlasting one. The full understanding of the divine dispensation will not be obtained in this life. Theology of the word, theology of earthly realities, theology of preaching, theology of signs, biblical theology, Church, Sacraments, are mere means to get some understanding of the divine realities for the time we walk by faith, not by sight, *"donec peregrinamur a Deo."* From this inadequacy of the human mind springs the need we experience of a living teaching.

Newman sets down a sixth principle: "It is our Lord's intention in His Incarnation to make us what He is Himself; this is the principle of *grace*, which is not only holy but sanctifying." Newman had first written: "A sixth [principle] is the sanctifying power (in action) as well as the sanctity itself, which is not only holy but sanctifying, which is involved in the idea of 'grace' as in those main (great) principles of revealed religion now enumerated."

In his *Lectures on Justification*—his most theological work—Newman explains at length the ancient doctrine of the indwelling not only of the Holy Spirit but of the world incarnate too, which from the time of the Fathers had been over-shadowed by the scholastic controversies of the sixteenth century. Against Protestants and against a certain decadent Catholic theology, which had lost contact with its proper sources, Newman's theology about increated grace, which is for him the first and last scope of the Incarnation, is to be found today among the most modern and learned theologians, and what is more, in the teaching of Pius XII, in the Encyclical Letters on the Mystical Body of Christ.

7. "It [Grace] cannot elevate and change us without mortifying our lower nature:—here is the principle of *asceticism*." Newman in his original draft expressed it as: "the principle of mortification, self-discipline, and self-sacrifice, according to our pattern."

Newman often affirmed that man is made by discipline; but by abnegation the Christian is made. It is not very often given to us to see in a single man the harmony we find in Newman's view of Christianity. The manifold aspects of Christian religion are put out with that singleness of purpose which is to be found only in those people who have realized their own unity first. Mind, heart, and conscience, whose divorce is the evil of every age, were in Newman so symbiotically joined that it is no wonder if his theology, his moral doctrine, and psychology were intended to grasp and realize for himself and others the whole of Christ.

8. "And, involved in this death of the natural man, is necessarily a revelation of the *malignity of sin,* in corroboration of the forebodings of conscience." The first redaction of the principle read more briefly: "Involved in this death, whether of our Lord or ours is a revelation of the unspeakable malignity of sin."

For the preacher of "The Cross, the measure of the World," the answer to the question proposed by the Psalmist: *Delicta, quis intelliget?* is to be found in our Lord's death and ours. So convinced was he of the malignity of sin—and he had no personal experience of a mortal sin during his long lifetime, as we may believe from the reading of his *Autobiographical Writings*—that the view of a sinful world around him was the most crucial difficulty he felt against the existence of God. "Were it not for this voice speaking so clearly in my conscience and my heart, I should be an atheist. . . ."

9. "Also by the fact of an Incarnation we are taught that matter is an essential part of us, and, as well as mind, is *capable of sanctification.*" "This principle," he wrote before, "has relation to the subject sanctified (of sanctification), after the (pattern) prototypical instance of the Incarnation, is matter as well as mind. Matter is in Christianity no evil in itself, not some necessary incumbrance or impediment to good. It is an essential part of us and is (altogether) capable of a spiritual change (transformation) fitting it for the eternal Presence of God."

"Development itself is such a principle." Preparing the

later edition of the essay on the *Development of Christian Doctrine,* he added this tenth principle in a footnote:

And thus I was led on to a further consideration. I saw that the principle of development not only accounted for certain facts, but was in itself a remarkable philosophical phenomenon, giving a character to the whole course of Christian thought. It was discernible from the first years of Catholic teaching up to the present day, and gave to that teaching a unity and individuality. It served as a sort of test, which the Anglican could not stand, that modern Rome was in truth ancient Antioch, Alexandria, and Constantinople, just as a mathematical curve has its own law and expression. *Apol.* p. 198, *vid.* also Angl. Diff. vol. i. Lect. xii. 7.[19]

The Incarnation was for Newman the pattern of every true development. Looking to our Lord growing "in wisdom, stature and favour" (Luke II, 52) and looking to the Church as a fact too in the world's history, Newman, instead of seeing—as many did—in the Church's changes during the centuries an argument against it, found in its development the very argument of its divine origin. "In a higher world it is otherwise, but here below to live is to change, and to be perfect is to have changed often." [20]

In 1845 Newman was received into the Church. He became a Catholic, not an atheist or a pantheist nor a polytheist. His second principle of 1833 was not changed with his conversion, but on the contrary, attained its full perfection and true reality: "Secondly, I was confident in the truth of a certain definite religious teaching, based upon this foundation of dogma; viz. that there was a visible Church, with sacraments and rites, which are the channels of invisible grace. I thought that this was the doctrine of Scripture, of the early Church, and of the Anglican Church. Here again, I have not changed my opinion; I am as certain now on this point as I was in 1833, and never have ceased to be certain." [21]

If he changed in 1845 it was in order to be the same. "I was not conscious of firmer faith in the fundamental truths of the Revelation, or of more self-command . . . but it was like coming into port after a rough sea. . . ." [22] He added something, he relinquished nothing. The last part of the *Apologia*, written six years before the definition of the Pope's infallibility, shows us Newman giving arguments from antecedent probabilities on behalf of papal infallibility. He was not in favor of the definition at that time. He defended it, however, when a call was made on him by Gladstone's attacks.

Supposing then it to be the Will of the Creator to interfere in human affairs, and to make provisions for retaining in the world a knowledge of Himself, so definite and distinct as to be proof against the energy of human scepticism, in such a case,—I am far from saying that there was no other way,—but there is nothing to surprise the mind, if He should think fit to introduce a power into the world, invested with the prerogative of infallibility in religious matters. Such a provision would be a direct, immediate, active, and prompt means of withstanding the difficulty; it would be an instrument suited to the need; and, when I find that this is the very claim of the Catholic Church, not only do I feel no difficulty in admitting the idea, but there is a fitness in it, which recommends it to my mind. [23]

The Church is one with our Lord, in time, by the Apostolical Succession; in space, by its Catholicity. By its holiness, it partakes of His own spirit. Under the shock of Wiseman's putting forward Augustine's sentence: "*Securus iudicat orbis terrarum*," Newman realized there was no

Catholicity in the Establishment. When the Bishops attacked Tract 90, he knew that the apostolical succession was not with them. Holiness was the only argument which kept Newman at Littlemore for some years more. He had the experience of holiness in the Church into which he was born. But he gained another experience in those days. If he wished to follow—as he had resolved in 1816 when he became a real man—the intimations of conscience, his guide of life, and so not sin against light—he could not remain in the Church of England.

In a paper entitled "An *Apologia* in brief," written to a lady who was to be received in the church the following year, 1872, the same theological implications that we tried to show in the foregoing pages can be discovered. The order is changed. Beginning with the church, it ends with conscience. In the light of it we ought to understand the famous passage in the Letter to the Duke of Norfolk, in which Newman toasts first conscience and then the Pope, for it is but another of Newman's expressions of St. Paul's sentence: *Quod non est ex fide, peccatum est.*

We should like to end this paper with that "*Apologia* in Brief," in which Newman presents a synthesis of his own theology:

As to your question, suggested by your friends, it is not at all the case that I left the Anglican Church from despair—but for two reasons concurrent, as I have stated in my *Apologia*—first, which I felt *before* any strong act had been taken against the Tracts or me, namely, in 1839, that the Anglican Church *now* was in the position of the Arian Churches of the fourth century, and the Monophysite Churches of the fifth, and this was such a shock to me that I at once made arrangements for giving up the editorship of the *British Critic*, and for a long time I contemplated giving up St. Mary's. This shock was the *cause* of my writing N. 90 which excited so much commotion. N. 90 which roused the Protestant world against me, most likely never would be written except for this shock. Thus, you see, my condemnation of the Anglican Church arose *not* out of despair, but when everything was hopeful, *out of my study of the Fathers.* Then, as to the second cause, it began in the autumn of 1841, six months after N. 90 when the Bishops began to charge against me. This brought home to me that I had *no business in the Anglican Church.* It was not that I despaired of the Anglican Church, but that opposition *confirmed* the interpretation which I had put upon the Fathers, that they *who loved the Fathers, could have* no place in the Church of England.

As to your further question, whether, *if* I had stayed in the Anglican Church *till now,* I should have joined the Catholic Church at all, at any time now or hereafter, I think that most probably I should *not;* but *observe,* for this reason, because God gives grace, and if it is not accepted, He withdraws His grace. Since, of His free mercy, and from no merits of mine, He then offered me the grace of conversion, if I had not acted upon it, it was to be expected that I should be left, a worthless stump, to cumber the ground and to remain where I was till I died.

Of course, you are endlessly bewildered by hearing and reading on both sides. What I should recommend you, if you ask me, is to put aside all controversy and close your ears to advocates on both sides for two months, and not open any controversial book, but to pray God to enlighten you continually, and then, at the end of the time, to find where you are. I think if you thus let yourself alone, or rather take care that others let yourself alone, you will at the end of the time see that you ought to be a Catholic. And if this is the case, it will be your duty at once to act upon this conviction. But if you go on reading, talking, being talked to, you will never have peace. God bless you, and guide you, and bring you safe into port.[24]

Becoming a Christian, Newman became a real man. Becoming a Catholic, he became a real Christian.

NOTES

1. *Letters and Correspondence of John Henry Newman during his Life in the English Church . . .* , ed. Anne Mozley (London, New York, and Bombay, 1903), I, 19.

2. *Grammar of Assent,* pp. 56–57.

3. *Apologia,* p. 108.

4. *Autobiographical Writings,* ed. Henry Tristram (New York, 1957), p. 150.

5. *Apologia,* p. 334.

6. *Grammar of Assent,* pp. 422–423.

7. *Apologia,* p. 291.

8. *Discourses Addressed to Mixed Congregations,* Sermon XIV.

9. *Apologia,* p. 336.

10. *Grammar of Assent,* p. 390.

11. *Stray Essays,* pp. 86–87.

12. *Apologia,* p. 150.

13. *Ibid.,* pp. 334–335.

14. *Meditations and Devotions* (London, 1894), pp. 125–126.

15. To S. Flanagan, Feb. 15, 1868. See *Gregorianum,* XXXIX (1958), 594.

16. *Essay on the Development of Christian Doctrine,* pp. 324–325. Subsequent quotations dealing with the principles that follow from the fact of the Incarnation are taken from this *Essay,* pp. 325–326, and from the original draft mentioned in note 17.

17. Birmingham Oratory Archives, D. 7. 6. In quoting from this draft, I have included erased words in parentheses.

18. *Summa Theologica*, II, II, 1, 2 ad 2.

19. *Development of Christian Doctrine*, p. 326n.

20. *Ibid.*, p. 40.

21. *Apologia*, p. 151.

22. *Ibid.*, p. 331.

23. *Ibid.*, p. 337.

24. Birmingham Oratory Archives. *Obituary Notices*, p. 10.

Jonathan Robinson: THE *Apologia* AND THE *Grammar of Assent*

The Apologia *is* the story of a man making up his mind, and the *Grammar of Assent* is the discussion of how people do make up their minds and of the value of such mind-making-up activities. The subtitle of the former is "A History of My Religious Opinions," which indicates well enough the subject matter of the book. Newman is concerned with vindicating his honesty, not with proving the validity of his conversion. "Let it be observed, that I am stating a matter of fact, not defending it; and if any Catholic says in consequence that I have been converted in the wrong way, I cannot help that now." He is concerned with describing, not defending, with outline, not explanation, and as a result the book taken by itself appears at times confusing or confused—depending on the reader—and seems the record of an emotional or a fideistic journey from one illiberalism to another.

The *Grammar of Assent* completes the argument of the *Apologia* by showing that the process of making up one's mind in matters of religion is not so very different from the way the mind works when it is operating on such mundane matters as buying a new suit or coming to the conclusion that Ethelbert is not to be trusted. Clearly, the first thing we wish to understand is how in fact the mind operates in thinking and reasoning; not, indeed, how the logic books may tell us it ought to act, but what experience, uncoerced by *à priori* theory, tells us is the case; nor do we wish to know the logical structure of the argument, but the movement of thought as it seeks truth in concrete matters. When we have done this, we will see first of all that the sort of arguments brought against making up our minds in matters of religion are equally valid in fields where the activity is essential and never questioned; and secondly, positively, that this way of acting is legitimate, and that only when the mind is so acting can it arrive at truth. The justification for the mind's acting so is that this is in fact the way it does operate, and this is sufficient ground for its validity. No one seriously doubts this when he attends to the daily business of living and forgets the abstractions and hesitations induced by the study of philosophy or by the acceptance of popular erroneous views of reason and proof.

To apply this to the *Apologia* we may say to begin with, that the record of Newman's conversion is the story of a man seeking truth about a complicated matter of fact, and finally making a judgment that certain things are in fact as the mind judges them to be. The validity of this process is guaranteed, because the process describes the only way the mind can operate in concrete matters when it sincerely pursues the truth. An argument presented solely in terms of deductions from principles would be no description of how Newman's mind or anyone else's could have operated, no matter how satisfying to our passion for the architectonic such a display of logical science might be.

In this paper I propose first to adumbrate the argument of the *Grammar of Assent,* and then to show how its principles are exemplified in the *Apologia.* Finally, I will make some observations on the effectiveness of the argument in the latter book.

I

The *Grammar of Assent* is not an easy book and for this reason I wish to begin with one or two remarks on the style and background of the work which will serve as an introduction to a more detailed examination of those points which concern us here.

In the first place the book is written in English of a very high order which avoids jargon and careless phrasing. If it is at times difficult to understand Newman it is because of the subject matter, not because he confuses obfuscation with profundity. The English language is a subtle instrument, and because the English philosophers have, on the whole, been great stylists, the apparent simplicity of their language has led many people outside the Anglo-Saxon tradition to underestimate their thought. This applies especially to Newman, as he is so often read by people who seem afflicted with a kind of passion to interpret his thought in a scholastic mode. He knew his Aristotle at first hand, but his expression of what he had learned from the philosopher is not that of one formed in the Roman schools. Yet this does not mean that he is not accurate, detailed, and quite as deep and difficult as those whose thought may be expressed in a more pretentious if less felicitous style.

In addition to the question of Newman's use of English there is the matter of the intellectual climate in which he was trained and in which he wrote. It was nineteenth-century Oxford that formed the man we are studying, and we ought to try to see Newman in this context before we begin calling him an existentialist or a personalist or a thomist or a nominalist or whatever. These may be useful exercises once we have grasped Newman's own point of view, but if we start anywhere else, distortion is inevitable. The understanding of the milieu in which a man writes helps us to understand the questions he was trying to answer. This in turn enables us to avoid a false perspective in our view of a writer, and it may also explain what seems to be false emphasis or distortion on his part.

Philosophy, and here I must be dogmatic to be brief, has two aspects: One of these we may call the doctrinal or historical and it is, however we understand the phrase, the *philosophia perennis*; while the other is dialectical or the aspect of dialogue. Without the first, philosophy loses its sense of direction and is in danger of foundering in a sea of triviality; without the second, it very quickly becomes an esoteric discipline with little relevance to the living currents of contemporary thought. It would be idle to deny that these two aspects of philosophy present a difficulty for the Christian philosopher. He may retreat to intellectual lucubrations on the transcendentals, or engage so wholeheartedly in dialogue that his philosophy becomes quite unconnected with his belief. The Christian who tries to remain faithful to both aspects—the *philosophia perennis* and dialogue—is not in for an easy time. It is, surely, one of Newman's many claims to genius that he remained faithful to a great tradition, which, through Bishop Butler, goes back to Aristotle, and at the same time expressed his thought in language that was living and apposite, language that the educated man of his day could understand.[1]

If, then, we approach Newman's theory without trying to make him into a scholastic or an empiricist or a nominalist, but endeavoring to understand what he actually says, we will find something like this. In the search for truth the progress of the mind has two quite distinct aspects or operations. One of these is what in ordinary language we call deciding or making up our minds, which Newman calls assent; the other is reasoning or thinking—making definitions, constructing hypotheses—everything that is not in fact assent.[2] He wants to make a clear distinction between: "Well yes, I see if I hold this I will be driven to holding that" and "yes this is the case, this is true." The first is hypothetical or conditional, the second is absolute and unconditioned. An appreciation of this distinction is vital if we are to understand Newman. It is more important than the distinction between notional and real assent which, although closely connected to this, is secondary. The former goes back to Aristotle, and we can find a modern treatment of it in Fr. Lonergan's *Insight* (New York, 1957).

This distinction is fundamental to any theory that is to escape the consequence, common to both absolute idealism and most forms of empiricism, that there can never be certainty about matters of fact. The root cause of this seemingly strange point of view is the theory of degrees of assent. It is the act of agreeing or assenting itself which varies, depending on a variety of factors. Once the notion of degrees of assent is admitted, it entails the consequence that any judgment about matters of faith is open to correction.

If we are to avoid degrees of assent, the categories of modality (that is of probability), existence and necessity, must be excluded from the act of judgment itself. Thus I may judge something to be probable, a matter of fact, or necessarily to be so, but in each case the act of judgment *quâ* act is the same. It is interesting to note that the nineteenth-century Scottish idealist Bernard Bosanquet criticized Newman for treating judgment in this way.

Bosanquet held that judgment is not a distinct unconditioned act, but that we affirm things to the degree to which we have evidence. "Thus assent becomes a sort of necessary shadow, following upon inference, which is the substance; and is never without some alloy of doubt, because inference in the concrete never reaches more than probability." [3] Newman, on the contrary, held it to be the teaching of experience that assent is an act *sui generis*, unconditioned, and not related to inference as a pale shadow to its object. This, Bosanquet complains, makes judgment into "an arbitrary and irrational activity. It is not surprising that in the *Grammar of Assent* ecclesiastical interest should have thrown itself zealously on the side of such a conception." [4]

This passage is interesting since it points up a very real problem: If judgment is an act that is different from inferring, collecting arguments, and making definitions, how can it be said to be rational? In a word, if reasoning is different from asserting, how then can asserting be anything other than the irrational and arbitrary activity of which Bosanquet spoke?

We find the point of view with which Newman disagrees stated in the *Grammar of Assent* with scrupulous fairness:

. . . at first sight it might seem as if Assent admitted of degrees, on account of the variation of vividness in these different apprehensions. As notions come of abstractions, so images come of experiences; the more fully the mind is occupied by an experience, the keener will be its assent to it, if it assents, and on the other hand, the duller will be its assent and the less operative, the more it is engaged with an abstraction; and thus a scale of assents is conceivable, either in the instance of one mind upon different subjects, or of many minds upon one subject, varying from an assent which looks like mere inference up to a belief both intense and practical,—from the acceptance which we accord to some accidental news of the day to the supernatural dogmatic faith of the Christian.[5]

Newman's position, however, is quite clearly the opposite, that the ground of the type of assent—notional or real—in no way affects the nature of the assent, "which is in all cases absolute and unconditional." This point of view, he believes, is the result of a true analysis of experience. If we treat the subject not according to "*à priori* fitness," but "according to the facts of human nature, as they are found in the concrete actions of life," we find numberless cases in which we do not assent at all, none in which assent is evidently conditional, and many in which it is unconditional, and in subject matters which admit of nothing higher than probable reasoning. Some of the examples that he analyzes are: the fact that we assent to our own existence, the fact that the world is a globe and the fact that "we laugh to scorn the idea that we had no parents though we have no memory of our birth; that we shall never depart this life, though we can have no experience of the future." [6] Locke himself, who held the doctrine of degrees of assent, contradicted himself flatly by admitting that we do assent in an unqualified way to many such propositions.

The next stop is to examine certitude, which is one sort of assent. Assent, as we all know to our sorrow, can be false; we can make up our minds too quickly, because of prejudice, because we have not considered the evidence, or because we are too stupid to cope properly with the situation. There are, however, assents that are true and known to be such, and in this case we have what Newman calls a certitude. To be a believer, as distinct from one who merely enquires about religion, one must have made assents that are at least capable of being turned into certitudes.

. . . Let the proposition to which the assent is given be as absolutely true as the reflex act pronounces it to be, that is, objectively true as well as subjectively:—then the assent may be called a *perception*, the conviction a *certitude*, the proposition or truth a *certainty*, or thing known, or a matter of *knowledge*, and to assent to it is to *know*.[7]

Certitude, then, is the perception of a truth with the perception that it is a truth.

There are two conditions of this certitude: the first of these is *à priori*, or from the nature of the case; and the second is *à posteriori*, or from experience. From the nature of the case, one of the main characteristics of certitude in any matter is to be confident that certitude will last, but also to be confident of this: that if it did fail, nevertheless, the thing itself, whatever it is, of which we are certain, will remain just as it is, true and irreversible. As far as the second condition goes, which we gain from our actual experience of certitude, we may say that it is a feeling that is specific and *sui generis*. In explaining this, Newman contrasts moral and aesthetic pleasure with that "relaxation and repose of mind which is characteristic of certitude." He contends that certitude is a normal and natural state of mind, and not (as is sometimes objected) one of its extravagancies of infirmities, and "as one would refuse to Inquiry, Doubt, and Knowledge a legitimate place among our mental constituents, so no one can reasonably ignore a state of mind which not only is shown to be substantive by possessing a sentiment *sui generis* and characteristic, but is analogical to Inquiry, Doubt, and Knowledge, in the fact of its thus having a sentiment of its own." [8]

The objections to this sort of argument are obvious, but as is usually the case, Newman states them better than his opponents:

. . . with the countless instances, on all sides of us, of human fallibility, with the constant exhibitions of antagonistic certitudes, who can so sin against modesty and sobriety of mind, as not to be content with probability, as the true guide to life, renouncing ambitious thoughts, which are sure either to delude him, or to disappoint. [9]

Newman analyzes this position with some care. First he distinguishes between certitude and infallibility. Infallibility is a gift which concerns a definite subject matter; certitude is a state of mind concerning one particular proposition. Thus the Pope, in declaring Our Lady's Assumption, exercised the gift of infallibility, but his state of mind in doing so was one of certitude. But although it is not infallibility, it does involve, as we have said, a sense of repose and security towards particular propositions consequent on investigation. But what, then, are we to say about mistakes? It must be remembered that certitude is a deliberate assent, given expressly on reason, and as a result, if the certitude is unfounded it is the reasoning which is at fault, not our assent to it. We cannot go against the facts. In reality, certitudes are part of our mental makeup and "mere abstract argument [is] impotent when directed against good evidence lying in the concrete." [10] An act is not wrong because it is done wrongly. False certitudes are faults because they are false, not because they are supposed certitudes. We don't dispense with clocks because they go wrong, and a watch may be organically perfect and still need regulating. Certitude then has its place amongst our mental acts, and the aberrations which may accompany the search for it in no way show the contrary.

Finally we have the question of how we can move from inference to assent, how it is that after a consideration of evidence or at times almost spontaneously we say "this is the case," "this is what I believe." How is it that we can make this passage from inquiry and inference to commitment? Here again we must pay attention to the deliverances of experience, and not to theory. We must remember that it is the mind, not language, which decides and makes disappear the margin between verbal argumentation and conclusions in the concrete. There is no kind of rule for this, because it is the mind in its living actual operation which has to decide for itself. This perfection of the operation of the mind, at least in concrete matters, Newman calls the illative sense. In a very interesting passage he affirms that this sense is an extension of Aristotle's doctrine of *phronesis* from the sphere of the practical intellect to the theoretical or truth-finding sphere. Thus, just as the test for moral action is the judgment of the man who acts wisely, so the test of the mind's searching for truth is the man who judges well.

The criterion, then, for the accuracy of the inference in concrete matters, is committed to the personal action of the ratiocinative faculty, the perfection or virtue of which is called the illative sense. "The certitude" which the operation of this sense leads to "is not a passive impression made on the mind from without, by argumentative compulsion, but in all concrete question . . . it is an active recognition of propositions as true." [11] Such certitudes can never be obtained from the logic of words, and since in concrete matters, at least, they are not merely the result of a scientific inquiry, it follows that they are the result of more fundamental if less formal, yet nonetheless legitimate, operations of the mind. "Every one who reasons, is his own centre; and no expedient for attaining a common measure of minds can reverse this truth." [12]

The most characteristic way the illative sense works is on the estimation of the convergence of probabilities. All we need to notice about this here is that the resulting assent is not therefore probable, but, given the proper working of the mind under its illative sense, is absolute and unconditioned.

The sanction of the sense is that we do in fact think in the fashion described by Newman. "We are in a world of facts, and we use them; for there is nothing else to use," and "It is enough for the proof of the value and authority of any function which I possess, to be able to pronounce that it is natural." "There is no ultimate test of truth besides the testimony born to truth by the mind itself, and that this phenomenon, perplexing as we may find it, is a normal and inevitable characteristic of the mental constitution of a being like man on a stage such as the world." [13]

The argument, then, of the *Grammar of Assent*, at least so far as it concerns us, is that truth is only attained by the act of assent or judgment. One of the species of assent is certitude, which is a truth known to be such, and, in concrete matters, the means by which the mind makes these judgments is the illative sense.

II

When we apply these principles to the *Apologia* we will be able to see how the earlier book exemplified principles that Newman was later to discuss in the *Grammar of Assent,* and at the same time our knowledge of the *Apologia* will help to clarify some of the difficulties of the foregoing discussion.

The *Grammar of Assent* is a discussion, as I have said, of how people make up their minds, and the answer is, in brief, by making up their minds. We can collect and arrange the rules of argument and proof, we can analyze the emotional, environmental, and hereditary factors at work in an individual, and then describe in detail the importance and the quality of the imagination as a factor in his thought. But to the extent that we say that making up our mind is identified with logical argument, emotional factors, or the imagination, to that extent have we failed to understand Newman's point, which is, to quote Bishop Butler, "everything is what it is and not another thing."

This in no way implies that logical discourse, emotional factors, and the imagination do not have their role in the mind's search for certainty; but it does mean that any attempt to "explain" the *Apologia* psychologically, whether in terms of Newman's imagination, or in terms of a succession of logical steps, is a mistake. To criticize Newman's account in *Apologia* for being "illogical" is to describe the conditions and concomitants of Newman's search for truth about a complicated matter of fact, not the search itself. It is to make what the English philosophers call a category mistake, and to forget the general principle that the mind is more versatile and vigorous than all its works, including language and, *à fortiori,* any of the many forces that may be presupposed by or accompany the assent to truth.

Any attempt to solve a problem, as distinct from explaining a solution, is done by an individual in certain definite circumstances, using the intellect, the emotional characteristics, and the imagination with which he has been endowed. The *Apologia* describes Newman's circumstances, and the other influences on his mind, whether they were arguments or emotional states or imagination, but these are not the same thing as his judgment that God wanted him to be a Catholic. The perception of this truth could not take place in abstraction from everything Newman was, but this is not to say that the truth that he recognized can in any way be explained away by what he was.

Newman tried to show that the mind has what may be termed informal ways of acting, which serve as the basis for any formal articulation of an argument. It is this informal reasoning or inference, which includes more factors than those of strict logical argument, which is governed by the illative sense. This sense operates in the actual conduct of the argument, in the selection of the elementary premises with which we start, and in the way the argument reaches a conclusion—not only, that is, the process of working towards an assent, but the assents we start with, as well as the final passage from inference to assent.

These three functions of the illative sense may become clearer if we apply them to the argument of the *Apologia;* but if we begin with the idea that the logic of words is the norm of the actual way the mind looks for truth we are sure to misunderstand Newman.

First of all there are the elementary principles with which we start an argument. Newman discusses these by

showing that fundamental contrarieties of opinion, in terms
of which a discussion is carried on, may be so deep as to
render dialogue almost impossible. This is because of the
differences of the particular aspects under which we view
a subject, that is, of our abstractions, which form our representative notions of what it is. Thus in the *Apologia* Newman describes some of the principles that underlay a good
part of his teaching; principles such as that of the sacramental economy, of probability as the guide to life, and of
the dogmatic character of religion.

These three notions were the spectacles through which
he saw all religious questions. He might have held the view
that dogma is the negation of all true religion, that nature
is absolutely corrupt and so in no way sacramental, or that
we have right only to act on mathematical or scientific
proof. Whatever the truth of the two sets of views may be,
they are so fundamentally opposed that discussion between
those who hold them becomes almost impossible. The formal
object, to use the scholastic term under which the material
is viewed, is so different in each case that what seems conclusive to one is hardly worthy of consideration by the
other. This kind of difference is what makes so much religious discussion a waste of time. It would be idle to pre-
tend that Newman's principles were the result of a kind of
deductive process. They were instead a tool which he
brought to religious discussion, the validity of which was
confirmed in the process of his investigation and the development of his experience.

Next we have the function of the illative sense during
the conduct of an argument. What counts for evidence for
one person does not seem to do so for another, and this too
is familiar to us from experience. It is not that the evidence
is not evidence in both cases; rather it is that what seems

to move one mind does not move another, or what has moved our mind at one time does not seem at another time to carry the same conviction. Newman describes this in a letter which he wrote to a friend before his conversion:

The *arguments* which I have published against Romanism seem to myself as cogent as ever, but men go by their sympathies, not by argument; and if I feel the force of this influence myself, who bow to the arguments, why may not others still more, who never have in the same degree admitted the arguments? [14]

This is a description of an experience with which we are all familiar. There is no point in saying the mind should not find itself changing this way: the fact is that it does. If Newman had been content merely to follow his sympathies, he would justly be condemned as an irrationalist; but it is patently clear from the *Apologia* that this is what he did *not* do. We are concerned here, however, with emphasizing the fact that the mind does seem to attach more weight to different arguments at different times, and this is because reasoning in concrete matters is not abstract, but is carried out into the realities of life, "its premises being instinct with the substance and the momentum of that mass of probabilities, which acting upon each other in correction and confirmation, carry it home definitely to the individual case which is its original scope." [15] Thus Newman saw that the Anglican Church, as he had worked it out, was a paper church, but the confrontation of the theory with the actual facts was not the work of a moment. The painful development of the idea under the pressure of diverse and varying circumstances was the work of years. Again, the process is more or less implicit: The movement of the mind, the shifting of perspective to accord with the growing appreciation of fact is imperceptible. The mind shifts and finds itself in a different position, and it is only upon reflection that it finds it has changed.

In the *Grammar*, Newman gives three examples of certitudes that are held on the basis of arguments that it would be difficult to adumbrate: the fact that Great Britain is an island, that we are certain Horace was not written in the thirteenth century, and the fact that we shall die. Our grounds for holding these, in so far as we can spell them out, are not the same as a logical defense of these propositions. Now many of our most reasonable and obstinate certainties are of this kind and depend on proofs that are informal and personal, which baffle our powers of analysis and cannot be brought under logical rule.

The perfection of informal inference, of this coming to certitudes that neither we nor anyone else denies, is, as we have seen, the work of the illative sense, which sees the pattern in a mass of fact, or the hidden clue in the tangled web of argument, and under whose guidance the mind assents to truth. From the time, when Newman first had serious doubts about Anglicanism, when he first saw his face in the mirror as that of a Monophysite, when Augustine's words *securus judicat orbis terrarum* first began to sound in his ears, he was to know no peace, because amongst the complex of fact and theory, hypothesis and certitude, his mind, under its illative sense, had run far ahead of its formal arguments. It was to take him several years before his presentiment that Rome would be shown to be right after all could be known with certainty, before the pattern that he suddenly discerned could be asserted with a reflex or reasoned assent. This was not to be his until he finally saw that his conversion at forty-five was the ineluctable conclusion of his turning to God at the age of fifteen.

This final activity of the illative sense, which determines the passage from inference to assents that are known to be true, is also the work of the mind, and, as a result, the assent to a fact may be as various as the many minds that make it; but it does not follow from this that because the ways are different they are invalid or improper, although this of course is possible in some cases. This is the crux of the matter. The acceptance of a thing as true is determined in practice by the living mind, which recognizes clues, straws in the wind, probabilities, which goes on to evaluate evidence and finally to assent to truth. The assent, to emphasize the point once again, is absolute and unconditional; not a high degree of probability, but an unqualified affirmation. It is not a case of "Oh my God, if there is a God, save my soul, if I have a soul." Nor is the point a kind of sophisticated anti-intellectualism, a short cut that excludes the necessity of hard thinking. What Newman is doing in the *Apologia* is describing as well as he can the different forces that in fact worked on his mind as he experienced his way to certitude, and in so doing he is describing the substratum of the arguments which can be expressed in language arranged as formal argument. He describes how he assented to the truth that the Church of Rome was the Church founded by the Son of God, and the process is rational, because it describes the living operation of Newman's mind operating according to its own nature. This process led him to the conclusion that there was no medium in true philosophy between atheism and catholicity, and that a perfectly consistent mind "under the circumstances which it finds itself here below," must embrace either the one or the other. "And I hold this still: I am a Catholic by virtue of my believing in God. . . ." [16]

III

Finally I wish to emphasize an aspect of the argument by asking a question. Why is it that the _Apologia_, being an account of a personal approach to the truth, can be said to be of any relevance to anyone but Newman himself—I mean beyond the immediate purpose of showing he was not a liar? The reason _in abstracto_ is that truth is not personal in the sense of being peculiar to the individual who discovers it. And though Newman's own experiences are enough for himself, and though he cannot lay down the law for others, nonetheless he does find that allowing for the difference of minds and of modes of speech, what convinces him will also convince others.

His true sobriety and modesty consists, not in claiming for his conclusions an acceptance or a scientific approval which is not to be found anywhere, but in stating what are personally his own grounds for his belief in Natural and Revealed religion,— grounds which he holds to be so sufficient, that he thinks that others do hold them implicitly or in substance, or would hold them, if they inquired fairly, or will hold if they listen to him, or do not hold from impediments, invincible or not as it may be, into which he has no call to inquire.[17]

But the fundamental reason why Newman's work is so effective is stated by himself in the _Grammar_. In concrete reasonings we judge for ourselves, by our own lights, and on our own principles; and our criterion of truth is not so much the manipulation of propositions as the intellectual and moral character of the person maintaining them, and the ultimate silent effect of his arguments and conclusions on our own minds.

This, surely, as so many have testified, is the effect of the *Apologia*. One of the main reasons for this impact is the manifest integrity of the writer. In this paper I have left aside the important question of conscience, as I wished to emphasize the distinction between assent and inference and the personal character of argument and of truth-seeking. But truth must be sought not only with the intellect but in the company of conscience. "Truth there is," Newman affirms, "and attainable it is, but . . . its rays stream in upon us through the medium of our moral as well as our intellectual being." [18] The perception of the first principles of truth is enfeebled and obstructed by sense and the supremacy of self, and only a man whose conscience keeps him at the job and refuses to allow him to accept pleasant or facile solutions will finally arrive at certitude.

In the end, Newman says, we trust people and not arguments, and the peculiar effectiveness of the *Apologia*, even today, is that it is the record of a man seeking and finding truth under the twin lights of genius and sanctity, and exemplifying in his own life the adherence under conscience to the truth where he found it, and as he found it, no matter what the cost to himself.

NOTES

1. The question as to how far his *ambiente* posed the subject matter of the questions he asked, as well as the substance of the answers, I must leave aside.

2. It is quite true that apprehension is treated as a separate category along with inference and assent; but it is common to both, or presupposed by both, rather than simply a third category.

3. *Grammar of Assent*, p. 159.

4. Bernard Bosanquet, *Logic or The Morphology of Knowledge* (Oxford, 1911), Second Edition, Book I, chapter 9.

5. *Grammar of Assent*, p. 35.

6. *Ibid.*, p. 178.

7. *Ibid.*, pp. 195–196.

8. *Ibid.*, p. 209.

9. *Ibid.*, pp. 223–224.

10. *Ibid.*, p. 232.

11. *Ibid.*, pp. 344–345.

12. *Ibid.*, p. 345.

13. *Ibid.*, pp. 346, 347, 350.

14. *Apologia*, p. 230.

15. *Grammar of Assent*, p. 292.

16. *Apologia*, p. 291.

17. *Grammar of Assent*, p. 386.

18. *Ibid.*, p. 311.

BIOGRAPHICAL NOTES ON
CONTRIBUTORS

The Reverend Hugo M. de Achaval, S.J., Professor of Sacred Theology at the Gregorian University, Rome, holds degrees in law and theology from Buenos Aires University, the Gregorian University, Rome, the University of San Miguel, Argentina. He has contributed articles on Newman to numerous professional journals and is currently editing Newman's unpublished theological papers.

Vincent Ferrer Blehl, S.J., Ph.D., Harvard University, is Associate Professor of English at Fordham University. With C. Stephen Dessain, he is the editor of Volumes XIV and XV of the *Letters and Diaries of John Henry Newman* (Thomas Nelson). He has also edited *The Essential Newman* (New American Library) and *Realizations: Newman's*

Selection of His Parochial and Plain Sermons (London: Darton, Longman and Todd).

William E. Buckler, Ph.D., University of Illinois, is Dean of the Washington Square College of Arts and Sciences, New York University, and editor of *The Victorian Newsletter*. His ten published works include *Matthew Arnold's Books: Toward a Publishing Diary* (Geneva: E. Droz), *Prose of the Victorian Period* (Houghton Mifflin), and *Novels in the Making* (Houghton Mifflin).

Francis X. Connolly, Professor of English at Fordham University, has been a member of the Fordham English Department since 1930. The author of numerous articles and books, his most recent publications are *Poetry: Its Power and Wisdom* (Scribner's), *The Wisdom of the Saints* (Pocket Books), *A Newman Reader* (Doubleday, Image Book), and *Man and His Measure* (Harcourt, Brace & World). With Vincent Ferrer Blehl, S.J., he is a co-director of the Fordham Center of Newman Studies. He is currently working on a biography of Newman.

Edward Kelly, S.J., born in Kirkwood, Missouri, received his B.S. and M.A. degrees from St. Louis University, and his Ph.D. degree in English from Fordham University in 1963. For his doctoral thesis he edited some of Newman's unpublished letters at the Oratory in Birmingham, England. At present he is pursuing theological studies at St. Mary's College, St. Marys, Kansas, in preparation for ordination to the priesthood.

Sister Mary Baylon Lenz, O.S.F., co-chairman of the English Department, Briar Cliff College, Sioux City, Iowa, received her M.A. and Ph.D. degrees from Notre Dame. Her doctoral dissertation, "Rhetorical Analysis of Newman's *Apologia Pro Vita Sua*," was a study of Newman's style.

Jonathan Robinson, Chaplain of the Newman Centre, Sir George Williams' University, Montreal, after receiving his Ph.D. degree in philosophy from Edinburgh University, became a Rockefeller Fellow at Oxford, 1954, and lectured in the Department of Logic and Metaphysics at Edinburgh, 1955 to 1957. He has written articles on Newman's philosophy for the *Downside Review* and the *Dublin Review*.

Martin J. Svaglic, Ph.D., University of Chicago, is Professor of English at Loyola University, Chicago. A specialist in Victorian literature, he has contributed essays on a variety of subjects to scholarly and other journals. He is the editor of Newman's *Idea of a University* (Holt, Rinehart & Winston), and of the forthcoming Oxford English Text edition of the *Apologia Pro Vita Sua*.

Sister Mary James McCormick, O.P.:

BIBLIOGRAPHY

The following is a selected bibliography including all works that are cited in the Symposium papers plus a few additional entries pertinent to a study of the *Apologia* under the various aspects with which this volume is concerned. For a more complete bibliography consult the following:

Cambridge Bibliography of English Literature. Vol. III (686–691).

Cardinal Newman-Studien, ed. H. Fries and W. Becker. 4 vols. Nurnberg, 1957.

Delattre, F. *La Pensée de John Henry Newman.* Paris, 1914 (297–302).

Guibert, J. *Le Reveil du Catholicisme en Angleterre au XIXe Siecle.* Paris, 1907 (315–335).

Guitton, J. *La Philosophie de Newman.* Paris, 1933 (195–230).

168

Harrold, Charles F. *John Henry Newman: An Expository and Critical Study of His Mind, Thought and Art.* London, 1945 (440–452).

Tristram, H. and Bacchus, F. "Newman," *Dictionnaire de Théologie Catholique.* Vol. XI. Paris, 1903–1949.

NEWMAN'S WORKS

(NOTE: Only the works cited in this volume are listed. Page references to the *Apologia* in all footnotes in the text are to the edition of Wilfrid Ward, Oxford University Press, 1913. Unless otherwise noted all other references are to the standard edition of Newman's works (40 volumes) published by Longmans Green and Co. (1874–1921). The dates of first publication of the individual works by Newman are given in parentheses below.)

Apologia Pro Vita Sua. The Two Versions of 1864 and 1865, ed. Wilfrid Ward. London, 1913.

Apologia Pro Vita Sua, ed. Charles F. Harrold. New York, 1947.

Apologia Pro Vita Sua. Modern Library Edition. Introduction by Anton C. Pegis. New York, 1950.

Apologia Pro Vita Sua, ed. A. Dwight Culler. Riverside Edition. Boston, 1956 (paperback).

Apologia Pro Vita Sua. Image Books Edition. Introduction by Philip Hughes. Garden City, New York, 1956 (paperback).

Discourses to Mixed Congregations (1849).

An Essay in Aid of a Grammar of Assent (1870).

Essay on the Development of Christian Doctrine (1845).

Historical Sketches. 3 vols. (1872–1873).

The Idea of a University (1852).

Lectures and Essays on University Subjects (1859).

Lectures on Certain Difficulties Felt by Anglicans in Catholic Teaching (1850).

Meditations and Devotions (1893).

On Consulting the Faithful in Matters of Doctrine, ed. John Coulson. New York, 1961. (*Rambler*, July, 1859.)

Oxford University Sermons (1843).

Sermons Preached on Various Occasions (1857).

LETTERS AND AUTOBIOGRAPHICAL WORKS

Cardinal Newman and William Froude, F.R.S.: A Correspondence, ed. Gordon H. Harper. Baltimore, 1933.

Correspondence of John Henry Newman with Keble and Others: 1839–1845, ed. at the Birmingham Oratory. London, 1917.

John Henry Newman: Autobiographical Writings, ed. Henry Tristram. London, 1956; New York, 1957.

Letters and Correspondence of John Henry Newman during his Life in the English Church, ed. Anne Mozley. 2 vols. London, 1891.

The Letters and Diaries of John Henry Newman, ed. Charles Stephen Dessain. Vols. XI, XII, XIII. London, 1961–1963.

BIOGRAPHICAL, CRITICAL, AND HISTORICAL REFERENCES

Altholz, Josef. *The Liberal Catholic Movement in England.* London, 1962.

American Quarterly Church Review, XVII (April, 1865), 661–685.

"Apologia pro Vita Sua," *Church and State Review* (August 1, 1864).

Aristotle. *The Rhetoric and Poetics of Aristotle*, trans. W. Rhys Roberts and Ingram Bywater. Modern Library Edition. New York, 1954.

Athenaeum (May 21, 1864).

"Authority and Free Thought: Dr. Newman's Apology," *Theological Review*, I (July, 1864), 306–334.

Benn, A. W. *History of English Rationalism.* 2 vols. London, 1906.

Bernard, E. D. *A Preface to Newman's Theology.* St. Louis, Missouri, 1945.

Bevington, Merle M. *The Saturday Review, 1855–1868.* . . . New York, 1941.

Boekraad, A. J. *The Personal Conquest of Truth.* Louvain, 1955.

Bosanquet, Bernard. *Logic or The Morphology of Knowledge.* Second Edition. Oxford, 1911.

Boston Review, V (January, 1865), 31–41.

Brinton, Crane. *English Political Thought in the Nineteenth Century.* London, 1933.

British Quarterly Review, XL (July 1, 1864), 102–126.

Buckler, William E. "A Dual Quest: The Victorian Search For Identity and Authority," *Arts and Sciences* (Spring, 1962), 27–33.

Burgum, E. B. "Cardinal Newman and the Complexity of Truth," *Sewanee Review,* XXXVIII (1930), 310–327.

Butler, Dom Cuthbert. *The Life and Times of Bishop Ulla-thorne.* 2 Vols. London, 1926.

Charles Kingsley: His Letters and Memories of His Life. Edited by His Wife. 2 vols. London, 1877.

Chesterton, Gilbert K. *The Victorian Age in Literature.* Notre Dame, 1962.

Church, R. W. *The Oxford Movement.* London, 1894.

Clerical Journal (July 7, 1864).

Colby, Robert. "The Poetical Structure of Newman's *Apologia Pro Vita Sua,*" *Journal of Religion,* XXXIII (January, 1953), 42–57.

———. "The Structure of Newman's *Apologia Pro Vita Sua* in Relation to His Theory of Assent," *Dublin Review,* CCXXVII (1953), 140–156.

Cross, Frank L. *John Henry Newman: With a Set of Unpublished Letters*. London, 1933.

Culler, A. Dwight. "Method in the Study of Victorian Prose," *Victorian Newsletter*, No. 9 (Spring 1956).

D'Achaval, Hugo M. "An Unpublished Paper by Cardinal Newman on the Development of Doctrine," *Gregorianum*, XXXIX (1958), 585–596.

Deen, L. W. "The Rhetoric of Newman's *Apologia*," *ELH*, XXIX (June, 1962), 224–238.

"Dr. Newman," *British and Foreign Evangelical Review*, XIII (October, 1864), 771–803.

"Dr. Newman and the Church of England," *Union Review*, II (July, 1864), 481–515.

"Dr. Newman and Mr. Kingsley," *Saturday Review*, XVII (February 27, 1864).

"Dr. Newman at Confession," *Evangelical Witness and Presbyterian Review*, III (September, 1864), 225–229.

"Dr. Newman's *Apologia*," *Evangelical Christendom*, XVIII (September 1, 1864), 421–428; (October 1, 1864), 477–482.

"Dr. Newman's *Apologia*," *Fraser's Magazine*, LXX (September, 1864), 265–303.

"Dr. Newman's *Apologia*," *London Quarterly Review* (Boston edition of *The Quarterly Review*, published in London), CXVI (October, 1864), 273–297.

"Dr. Newman's *Apologia*," *London Review* (June 25, 1864).

"Dr. Newman's *Apologia*," *Westminster Review* (American edition), LXXXII (September, 1864), 168–177.

"Dr. Newman's *Apologia pro Vita Sua*," *Christian Observer*, LXXIII (September, 1864), 661–685.

"Dr. Newman's Apology," *The Christian Remembrancer*, XLVIII (July, 1864), 162–193.

"Dr. Newman's Apology," *Spectator* (June 4, 1864).

"Dr. Newman's Apology," *Weekly Review* (June 25, 1864).

"Dr. Newman's Autobiography," *Ecclesiastic*, XXVI (July, 1864), 310–325.

Fairbairn, A. M. *Catholicism: Roman and Anglican*. London, 1889.

Folghera, J. D. *Newman's Apologetic*, trans. Philip Hereford. London, 1930.

Fothergill, Brian. *Nicholas Wiseman*. Garden City, New York, 1963.

Froude, James A. *The Nemesis of Faith*. Second Edition. London, 1849.

Gates, Lewis E. *Selections from the Prose Writings of John Henry Cardinal Newman*. New York, 1895.

Gosse, Edmund. *English Literature: An Illustrated Record*. New York, 1923.

Houghton, Walter E. *The Art of Newman's "Apologia."* New Haven, 1945.

Hutton, Richard H. *Cardinal Newman*. London, 1905.

———. "Father Newman's Sarcasm," *Spectator* (February 20, 1864).

Hutton, W. H. "The Oxford Movement," *Cambridge History of English Literature*, Vol. XII. Cambridge, 1946 (280–308).

Inge, W. R. "Cardinal Newman," *Outspoken Essays: First Series*. London, 1919.

Inquirer (June 18, 1864).

[Irons, William J.] *"Apologia Pro Vitâ" Ecclesiae Anglicanae*. London, 1864.

"J. H. Newman's *Apologia*," *North British Review*, XLI (August, 1864), 85–104.

John Bull (July 23, 1864).

"John Henry Newman," *The Patriot* (July 21, 1864).

Kelly, Edward, S.J. "Cardinal Newman's Unpublished Letters: A Selection from the Year July, 1864 to July, 1865." Unpublished doctoral dissertation, Fordham University, 1963.

Kendall, Guy. *Charles Kingsley and His Ideas*. London, 1947.

Leslie, Shane. *Henry Edward Manning: His Life and Labours*. London, 1921.

Liddon, H. P. *Life of E. B. Pusey*. 4 vols. London, 1893–1897.

Lilly, W. S. "Newman," *Dictionary of National Biography*, Vol. 14. New York, 1909 (340–351).

Life and Works of Charles Kingsley. 19 vols. London, 1901.

Literary History of England, ed. A. C. Baugh, *et al.* New York, 1948.

Loughery, James H. "Rhetorical Theory of John Cardinal Newman." Unpublished doctoral dissertation. University of Michigan, 1951.

MacDougall, Hugh A. *The Acton-Newman Relations*. New York, 1962.

Manning, Henry E. *England and Christendom*. London, 1867.

Martin, Robert B. *The Dust of Combat*. London, 1959.

Morrison, J. L. "The Oxford Movement and the British Periodicals," *Catholic Historical Review*, XLV (July, 1959), 137–160.

Ms *Apologia* Letters. 3 vols. Birmingham Oratory Archives.

Ms Pusey Letters, 1860–1864. Birmingham Oratory Archives.

"Newman," *Oxford Companion to English Literature*, ed. Sir Paul Henry. Oxford, 1946.

Newman, Francis W. *Phases of Faith*. London, 1870.

Newman: Prose and Poetry, ed. Geoffrey Tillotson. Cambridge, Mass., 1957.

The Norton Anthology of English Literature, ed. G. H. Ford, New York, 1962.

Obituary Notices. Birmingham Oratory Archives.

"Personal Attacks, 1834–1883." Birmingham Oratory Archives.

Pett, Douglas E. "The Newman-Kingsley Dispute Continues," *Times Literary Supplement* (17 February 1961), p. xvi; C. Stephen Dessain, 24 February, p. 121 and Mr. Pett's rejoinder, 3 March, p. 137; Edward Kelly, S.J., 10 March, p. 153 and Mr. Pett's rejoinder, 17 March, p. 169.

Philosophical Readings in Cardinal Newman, ed. James Collins. Chicago, 1961.

The *Press* (June 11, 1864); (July 16, 1864).

Purcell, Edmund S. *Life of Cardinal Manning*. 2 vols. London, 1895.

Reilly, J. J. *Newman As a Man of Letters*. New York, 1925.

"Rev. Charles Kingsley and Dr. Newman," *Blackwood's Edinburgh Magazine*, XCVI (September, 1864), 292–308.

Robertson, Thomas L., Jr. "The Kingsley-Newman Controversy and the *Apologia*," *MLN*, LXIX (1954), 564–569.

"Roman Catholic Casuistry and Protestant Prejudice," *Spectator* (March 26, 1864).

Ryan, Alvan S. "Newman's Conception of Literature," *Critical Studies in Arnold, Emerson and Newman*, ed. J. E. Baker. University of Iowa Humanistic Studies, VI, No. 1. Iowa City, 1942.

Shumaker, Wayne. *English Autobiography: Its Emergence, Material and Form*. University of California Publications in English. Berkeley, 1954.

Stephen, Leslie. *An Agnostic's Apology*. London, 1903.

———. "Charles Kingsley," *Dictionary of National Biography*, Vol. 11. New York, 1901 (175–181).

Svaglic, Martin J. "Method in the Study of Victorian Prose: Another View," *Victorian Newsletter*, No. 11 (Spring, 1957).

Svaglic, Martin J. "Newman's *Apologia Pro Vita Sua*: Intro-duction, Notes, and Commentary." Unpublished doctoral dissertation. University of Chicago, 1949.

————. "The Revision of Newman's *Apologia*," *Modern Philology*, L (August, 1952), 43–49.

————. "The Structure of Newman's *Apologia*," PMLA, LXVI (1951), 138–148.

Tardivel, Fernande. *La Personalité Littéraire de Newman*. Paris, 1937.

Thackeray, William M. *The History of Pendennis*. 2 vols. London, 1884.

Thomas Aquinas, *Summa Theologica*, Ottawa, 1941.

Thorp, Margaret Farrand. *Charles Kingsley*. Princeton, 1937.

The *Times* (February 26 and 27, 1863).

Trevor, Meriol. *Newman: Light in Winter*. New York, 1963.

————. *Newman: The Pillar of the Cloud*. New York, 1962.

Tristram, Henry. "Note au bas d'un grand texte," *La France Franciscaine*, IIIe serie, XXII (Janvier-Mars, 1939), 35–48.

Union Review, II (October, 1864), 506–517.

Victorian Literature, ed. A. Wright. New York, 1961.

Walgrave, J. H. *Newman the Theologian*, trans. A. V. Little-dale. New York, 1960.

Ward, Wilfrid. *Last Lectures*. London, 1918.

————. *The Life of John Henry Cardinal Newman based on his Private Journals and Correspondence*. 2 vols. London, 1912.

Wilberforce, Samuel. "Dr. Newman's *Apologia*," *Quarterly Review*, CXVI (October, 1864), 528–573.

Wright, C. "Newman and Kingsley," *Harvard Graduates' Magazine*, XL (December, 1931), 127–134.

INDEX

177